RISIN

RISING SIGNS

Discover the Truth about Your Personality

Sasha Fenton

Thorsons
An Imprint of HarperCollins*Publishers*

Thorsons
An Imprint of HarperCollins*Publishers*
77–85 Fulham palace Road,
Hammersmith, London W6 8JB
1160 Battery Street,
San Francisco, California 94111–1213

First published by The Aquarian Press 1989
Thorsons edition 1995
7 9 10 8

A catalogue record for this book
is available from the British Library

ISBN 0 85030 751 1

Printed in Great Britain by
HarperCollins Manufacturing Glasgow

Contents

Acknowledgments

I gratefully acknowledge my long suffering family, Tony, Helen and Stuart Fenton, for all their help and encouragement.

Grateful thanks to Frank Anderson for correcting my manuscript for me, and to Malcolm Wright for illustrations.

With a special thank you to Denise Russell.

> The Ram, the Bull, the Heavenly Twins,
> And next the Crab, the Lion shines,
> The Virgin, and the Scales,
> The Scorpion, Archer, and He-Goat,
> The Man that bears the Watering-Pot,
> And Fish with glittering tails.
>
> Anon.

Dedication

This book is dedicated to Sandra Richards who made me look closely at the subject of astrology in general, and the ascendant in particular, all those years ago.

Introduction

This book is intended to help you understand the significance of the ascendant and the rising sign. If you enjoyed my book *Moon Signs* you will enjoy this one as well because it looks at the rising sign in the same way as the previous book looked at the Moon. I have taken almost all my information from what an academically-minded friend calls 'original research'. This means that I have used my experience of observing people in the light of their birthcharts over many years in addition to the information which resulted from a series of questionnaires which I handed out to all and sundry. I have used other books on occasion in order to check up on some fact or other and you will find a list of these in the bibliography section.

I would like to mention that this book has taken fifteen years to come into being, because that is the length of time during which I have been fascinated by the ascendant. My fascination began when a very gifted astrologer called Sandra Richards called my attention to the importance of the rising sign and gave me her interpretations of its effect on our personalities. I lost touch with Sandra shortly after conversation and never had the opportunity to thank her for inspiring me. Sandra, if you read this book, you will find that the information which you gave me has stood the test of time. Those ideas are still alive and kicking, they are expressed in this book along with my own research and experience over the intervening years.

PART ONE
Background

CHAPTER 1

The Rising Sign

The rising sign is the sign which is passing over the horizon at the time of the subject's birth. The actual point where the zodiac sign passes upwards over the horizon is called the *ascendant*. This sign has a strong modifying effect on the personality. It frequently governs the subject's outer manner and modifies his mental outlook; it explains much of his behaviour to others, especially in impersonal situations. This sign often represents the *public face* of the subject; in other words, the image which he displays to those outside his home environment. This image may be part and parcel of his normal personality or it may be a carefully constructed mask. To some extent this side of the personality is under the subject's own control, which suggests that he can adapt it to fit different circumstances at various stages of his life. However, even the *way* he seeks to change his image is strongly influenced by the rising sign. Nothing in astrology is cut and dried, there are many people who are exceptions to these rules. In some cases there may be technical reasons for someone having an apparently weak rising sign.

The ascendant represents the moment of birth, and the sign which it occupies is associated with one's earliest experiences of life. When one looks at the old and fascinating argument of whether heredity or environment is the stronger influence on a personality, the rising sign gives valuable clues to the

environmental factors, whilst the arrangement of the planets
and the signs in which they are placed would fill in the bulk
of the genetic information. These observations have to be
weighed carefully when looking at each individual person
and each individual birthchart but even so, the rising sign
will throw a great deal of light on the early programming
which affects a subject's manners and behaviour in various
situations.

One can argue that the ascendant represents the kind of
person our parents and teachers wanted us to be, while the Sun,
Moon and other planets show the true self. This would account
for the fact that we tend to project the ascendant when we are
unsure of ourselves. The ascendant may act as a shield which
hides and protects the real personality, thereby allowing us to
assess any new situation before relaxing and revealing our true
feelings. The opposite point to the ascendant on a birthchart is
the *descendant*, and this gives an interesting insight into the kind
of person to whom we are attracted.

Appearance
The sign on the ascendant frequently modifies a subject's
appearance. Some people look far more like their rising sign
than their Sun sign, while others are a mixture of both.
However, there are people whose appearance is strongly
influenced by other factors on their birthchart. Astrologers who
suggest that all those who have Aries rising automatically have
round faces and red hair can run into trouble. What if the
subject were a Mshona tribesman from Zimbabwe? If the
tribesman had a strongly Arian chart plus an Aries ascendant, he
probably would have a round face and would also be small,
stocky and fierce, but what chance of red hair? Appearance is
therefore relative and must be considered against the background of race and family likeness.

Several years ago I read of a survey which had been carried
out with 100 subjects. About 45 per cent looked like their Sun
sign and about another 40 per cent resembled their rising sign
while the remainder looked like either their Moon sign or the
sign in which their chart ruler* was placed. I'm not sure that one

survey of 100 people proves much, but it is interesting all the same. It is possible that the outward projection of the rising sign is more apparent in our mannerisms and our outward behaviour than our looks. I have noticed that whenever I or any other astrologer has been daft enough to try to guess a person's Sun sign, we invariably come up with their rising sign instead.

It is always interesting to take a look at a family group to see how the signs are distributed within it. So often one finds that the Sun sign of one person becomes the rising sign of another and the Moon sign or the mid-heaven of yet a third. It is also interesting to note the factors on the birthcharts of people whom we choose as close associates of one kind or another to see whether they are drawn to our ascendant/descendant cusps or those of our MC/IC**

————————What Is A Rising Sign?————————

Technically speaking, the rising sign is the sign of the zodiac which is rising over the horizon at the time of birth. Less technically speaking, let us try to imagine the break of day when the Sun and the eastern horizon (the ascendant) are at the same point. By noon the Sun will be overhead and at dusk the Sun will be on the opposite side to the eastern horizon. Remember that the Earth revolves around the Sun once every 24 hours, therefore the Sun and the corresponding 'Sun sign' will be in a different position at different times of the day.

As the Earth turns all the way round once in 24 hours, the ascendant appears to travel through each one of the 12 signs of the zodiac once in each complete 24-hour day.

The ascendant is the starting point of a birthchart. It is the point where the first house begins with the other 11 houses following on around the chart. This means that the various

* The planet which is associated with the rising sign. Therefore, if Aries were rising the chart ruler would be Mars whilst if Virgo were rising the chart ruler would be Mercury.

** The abbreviation MC stands for medium coeli which is another term for the mid-heaven, which is at the top of the chart, while the term IC refers to the immum coeli or nadir which is at the bottom of the chart.

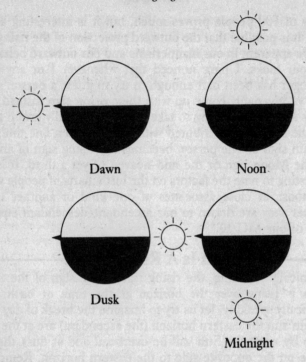

Dawn   Noon

Dusk

Midnight

Figure 1: The sun's passage in relation to the ecliptic (▲)

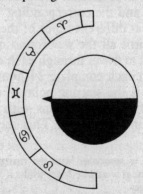

Figure 2: The signs of the zodiac rising up over the ecliptic; in this
case, the rising sign is Gemini

planets will be assigned to their own particular **houses** according to the **time** of birth, whilst they are assigned to their various **signs** according to the **date** of birth.

Variations in influence of the ascendant on a birthchart

The rising sign is not the only modifying force in a birthchart. A grouping of planets, usually called a *stellium*, placed in one sign or house will have a strong effect. The angles between the planets which are called *aspects* will also have an influence. However, there are a couple of other factors which may cause the ascendant to be a stronger or weaker force in the chart.

a) **Strong ascendants**: There are 30° in each sign, these run from 0° to 29° respectively. If the ascendant is placed towards the beginning of a sign, most of the first house will be in that same sign. If the ascendant falls late in a sign, most of the first house will fall into the next sign and thus weaken the effect of the ascendant's power.

b) **Weak Suns**: The Sun is in a weak position when it is at the bottom of the chart, near the immum coeli (also called the IC, the nadir or the cusp of the fourth house). This is because the Sun was literally far away on the other side of the Earth when the subject was born, hidden from view and weakened in influence. The seventh and twelfth houses are also somewhat weak placements for the Sun whilst an unaspected Sun would probably be overshadowed by other factors on the chart.

Signs of long and short ascension

During the course of a 24-hour day, all 12 signs of the zodiac cross the ecliptic. In the tropics they do this more or less in neat two hourly intervals but the further away one moves from the equator the more distorted this movement becomes. This means that in Great Britain, we can have up to two and three-quarter hours during which the sign of Cancer is passing upwards over the ecliptic, whereas there could be little more than half an hour for Pisces to rise. In our part of the world, it is far easier to find people who have the longer ascension signs of Cancer and Leo rising than the shorter ascension signs of Pisces or Aries. In southern hemisphere countries the situation is different but not quite the reverse. There the signs of longest ascension are Capricorn and Aquarius, while the shorter signs are Virgo and Libra.

Do we grow out of our rising sign?

There is a popular theory that many people are far more like their Moon sign or their rising sign during the first 30 years of their lives, becoming more like their Sun sign later on. Another theory is that the progression of the ascendant from one sign to the next weakens the influence and allows the subject to grow and change. These are both worthwhile theories but like everything else in astrology, they have to be looked at against the birthchart as a whole and used alongside the application of both common sense and intuition.

CHAPTER 2

How to Find Your Ascendant

The easy way out

If you are completely turned off by the thought of any kind of chart calculation then do not despair. Most astrologers will be happy to supply you with a chart and a list of your planetary positions including your ascendant, descendant, mid-heaven and nadir. As long as you only require the figure work to be done and do not ask to have a chart interpreted as well, the fee should be minimal. Many astrologers these days use computers in order to remove the chore of calculating and they would be quite happy to run the figures off for you.

A quick way to find your ascendant for yourself

This method will work for births in the United Kingdom and for those in countries which are nearby, such as France and the Low Countries. Remember that the nearer the subject is born to Greenwich, the greater the accuracy of the method.

a) Look at Figure 3 (page 20) to see whether British Summer Time or Double Summer Time were operating when you were born.

b) Take a look at the table of figures on pages 21-24. Find your date of birth in the list on the left.

c) Look along the lines to find your exact time of birth. The zodiac sign at the top of the column will be your rising sign.

Figure 3: British Summer Times

Changing at 2 a.m., GMT

1916	21 May	–	1 Oct.	*1947	16 Mar.	–	2 Nov.
1917	8 Apr.	–	17 Sep.	1948	14 Mar.	–	31 Oct.
1918	24 Mar.	–	30 Sep.	1949	3 Apr.	–	30 Oct.
1919	30 Mar.	–	29 Sep.	1950	16 Apr.	–	22 Oct.
1920	28 Mar.	–	25 Oct.	1951	15 Apr	–	21 Oct.
1921	3 Apr.	–	3 Oct.	1952	20 Apr.	–	26 Oct.
1922	26 Mar.	–	8 Oct.	1953	19 Apr	–	4 Oct.
1923	22 Apr.	–	16 Sep.	1954	11 Apr.	–	3 Oct.
1924	13 Apr.	–	21 Sep.	1955	17 Apr.	–	2 Oct.
1925	19 Apr.	–	4 Oct.	1956	22 Apr.	–	7 Oct.
1926	18 Apr.	–	3 Oct.	1957	14 Apr.	–	6 Oct.
1927	10 Apr.	–	2 Oct.	1958	20 Apr.	–	5 Oct.
1928	22 Apr.	–	7 Oct.	1959	19 Apr.	–	4 Oct.
1929	21 Apr.	–	6 Oct.	1960	10 Apr.	–	2 Oct.
1930	13 Apr.	–	5 Oct.	1961	26 Mar.	–	29 Oct.
1931	19 Apr.	–	4 Oct.	1962	25 Mar.	–	28 Oct.
1932	17 Apr.	–	2 Oct.	1963	31 Mar.	–	27 Oct.
1933	9 Apr.	–	8 Oct.	1964	22 Mar.	–	25 Oct.
1934	22 Apr.	–	7 Oct.	1965	21 Mar.	–	24 Oct.
1935	14 Apr.	–	6 Oct.	1966	20 Mar.	–	23 Oct.
1936	19 Apr.	–	4 Oct.	1967	19 Mar	–	29 Oct.
1937	18 Apr.	–	3 Oct.	1968	from 18 Feb.		
1938	10 Apr.	–	2 Oct.		to 31 Oct. 1971		
1939	16 Apr.	–	19 Nov.	1972	19 Mar.	–	29 Oct.
1940	25 Feb.	–	31 Dec.	1973	18 Mar.	–	28 Oct.
*1941	1 Jan.	–	31 Dec.	1974	17 Mar.	–	27 Oct.
*1942	1 Jan.	–	31 Dec.	Thereafter, from 2 a.m. GMT on			
*1943	1 Jan.	–	31 Dec.	the day following the third Saturday			
*1944	1 Jan.	–	31 Dec.	in March until 2 a.m. GMT on the			
*1945	1 Jan.	–	7 Oct.	day following the fourth Sunday in			
1946	14 Apr.	–	6 Oct.	October.			

*Double Summer Time

1941	5 Apr.	–	9 Aug.	1944	4 May	–	10 Aug
1942	4 Apr.	–	15 Aug.	1945	2 Apr.	–	15 Jul.
1943	2 Apr.	–	17 Sep.	1947	13 Apr.	–	10 Aug.

Figure 4: Ascendant table

Birthdate		Aries	Taurus	Gemini
ARIES	21 to 31 Mar. 1 to 10 Apr. 11 to 20 Apr.	5.30am to 6.29am 5am to 5.59 am 4.15am to 5.14am	6.30am to 7.44am 6am to 7.14am 5.15am to 6.29am	7.45am to 9.29am 7.15am to 8.59 am 6.30am to 8.14am
TAURUS	21 to 30 Apr. 1 to 10 May 11 to 21 May	3.30am to 4.29am 3am to 3.59am 2.30am to 3.29am	4.30am to 5.44am 4am to 5.14am 3.30am to 4.44am	5.45am to 7.29am 5.15am to 6.59am 4.45am to 6.29am
GEMINI	22 to 31 May 1 to 10 Jun. 11 to 21 Jun.	2am to 2.59am 1.30am to 2.29am 12.45am to 1.44am	3am to 4.14am 2.30am to 3.44am 1.45am to 2.59am	4.15am to 5.59am 3.45am to 5.29am 3am to 4.44am
CANCER	22 to 30 Jun. 1 to 11 Jul. 12 to 22 Jul.	12am to 12.59am 11.30am to 12.29am 11pm to 11.59pm	1am to 2.14am 12.30am to 1.44am 12am to 1.14am	2.15am to 3.59am 1.45am to 3.29am 1.15am to 2.59am
LEO	23 to 31 Jul. 1 to 11 Aug. 12 to 23 Aug.	9.45am to 10.44pm 9.15am to 10.14pm 8.30pm to 9.29pm	10.45pm to 11.59pm 10.15pm to 11.29pm 9.30pm to 10.44pm	12am to 1.44am 11.30pm to 1.14am 1045pm to 12.29am
VIRGO	24 to 31 Aug. 1 to 11 Sep. 12 to 22 Sep.	7.30pm to 8.29pm 7pm to 7.59pm 6.15pm to 7.14pm	8.30pm to 9.44pm 8pm to 9.14pm 7.15pm to 8.29pm	9.45pm to 11.29pm 9.15pm to 10.59pm 8:30pm to 10.14pm
LIBRA	23 to 30 Sep. 1 to 11 Oct. 12 to 23 Oct.	5.30pm to 6.29pm 5pm to 5.59pm 4.15pm to 5.14pm	6.30pm to 7.44pm 6pm to 7.14pm 5.15pm to 6.29pm	7.45pm to 9.29pm 7.15pm to 8.59pm 6.30pm to 8.14pm
SCORPIO	24 to 31 Oct. 1 to 11 Nov. 12 to 22 Nov.	3.30pm to 4.29pm 2.45pm to 3.44pm 2.15pm to 3.14pm	4.30pm to 5.44pm 3.45pm to 4.59pm 3.15pm to 4.29pm	5.45pm to 7.29pm 5pm to 6.44pm 4.30pm to 6.14pm
SAGITTARIUS	23 to 30 Nov 1 to 11 Dec. 12 to 21 Dec.	1.30pm to 2.29pm 12.45pm to 1.44pm 12.15pm to 1.14pm	2.30pm to 3.44pm 1.45pm to 2.59pm 1.15pm to 2.29pm	3.45pm to 5.29pm 3pm to 4.44pm 2.30pm to 4.14pm
CAPRICORN	22 to 31 Dec. 1 to 11 Jan. 12 to 20 Jan.	11.15am to 12.14pm 10.45am to 11.44am 10.15am to 11.14am	12.15pm to 1.29pm 11.45am to 12.59pm 11.15am to 12.29pm	1.30pm to 3.14pm 1pm to 2.44pm 12.30pm to 2.14pm
AQUARIUS	21 to 31 Jan. 1 to 10 Feb. 11 to 18 Feb.	9.30am to 10.29am 9am to 9.59am 8.15am to 9.14am	10.30am to 11.44am 10am to 11.14am 9.15am to 10.29am	11.45am to 1.29pm 11.15am to 12.59pm 10.30am to 12.14pm
PISCES	19 to end Feb. 1 to 10 Mar. 11 to 20 Mar.	7.30am to 8.29am 7.15am to 8.14am 6.30am to 7.29am	8.30am to 9.44am 8.15am to 9.29am 7.30am to 8.44am	9.45am to 11.29am 9.30am to 11.14am 8.45am to 10.29am

Rising Signs

	Birthdate	Cancer	Leo	Virgo
ARIES	21 to 31 Mar. 1 to 10 Apr. 11 to 20 Apr.	9.30am to 11.59am 9am to 11.29am 8.15am to 10.44am	12pm to 2.44pm 11.30am to 2.14pm 10.45am to 1.29pm	2.45pm to 5.29pm 2.15pm to 4.59pm 1.30pm to 4.14pm
TAURUS	21 to 30 Apr. 1 to 10 May 11 to 21 May	7.30am to 9.59am 7am to 9.29am 6.30am to 8.59am	10am to 12.44pm 9.30am to 12.14pm 9am to 11.44am	12.45pm to 3.29pm 12.15pm to 2.59pm 11.45am to 2.29pm
GEMINI	22 to 31 May 1 to 10 Jun. 11 to 21 Jun.	6am to 8.29am 5.30am to 7.59am 4.45am to 7.14am	8.30am to 11.14am 8am to 10.44am 7.15am to 9.59am	11.15am to 1.59pm 10.45am to 1.29pm 10am to 12.44pm
CANCER	22 to 30 Jun. 1 to 11 Jul. 12 to 22 Jul.	4am to 6.29am 3.30am to 5.59am 3am to 5.29am	6.30am to 9.14am 6am to 8.44am 5.30am to 8.14am	9.15am to 11.59am 8.45am to 11.29am 8.15am to 10.59am
LEO	23 to 31 Jul. 1 to 11 Aug. 12 to 23 Aug.	1.45am to 4.14am 1.15am to 3.44am 12.30am to 2.59am	4.15am to 6.59am 3.45am to 6.29am 3am to 5.44am	7am to 9.44am 6.30am to 9.14am 5.45am to 8.29am
VIRGO	24 to 31 Aug. 1 to 11 Sep. 12 to 22 Sep.	11.30pm to 1.59am 11pm to 1.29am 10.15pm to 12.44am	2am to 4.44am 1.30am to 4.14am 12.45am to 3.29am	4.45am to 7.29am 4.15am to 6.59am 3.30am to 6.14am
LIBRA	23 to 30 Sep. 1 to 11 Oct. 12 to 23 Oct.	9.30pm to 11.59pm 9 to 11.29pm 8.15pm to 10.44pm	12am to 2.44am 11.30pm to 2.14am 10.45pm to 1.29am	2.45pm to 5.29pm 2.15pm to 4.59pm 1.30pm to 4.14pm
SCORPIO	24 to 31 Oct. 1 to 11 Nov. 12 to 22 Nov.	7.30pm to 9.59pm 6.45pm to 9.14pm 6.15pm to 8.44pm	10pm to 12.44am 9.15pm to 11.59pm 8.45pm to 11.29pm	12.45am to 3.29am 12am to 2.44am 11.30pm to 2.14am
SAGITTARIUS	23 to 30 Nov. 1 to 11 Dec. 12 to 21 Dec.	5.30pm to 7.59pm 4.45pm to 7.14pm 4.15pm to 6.44pm	8pm to 10.44pm 7.15pm to 9.59pm 6.45pm to 9.29pm	10.45pm to 1.29am 10pm to 12.44am 9.30pm to 12.14am
CAPRICORN	22 to 31 Dec. 1 to 11 Jan. 12 to 20 Jan.	3.15pm to 5.44pm 2.45pm to 5.14pm 2.15pm to 4.44pm	5.45pm to 8.29pm 5.15pm to 7.59pm 4.45pm to 7.29pm	8.30pm to 11.14pm 8pm to 10.44pm 7.30pm to 10.14pm
AQUARIUS	21 to 31 Jan. 1 to 10 Feb. 11 to 18 Feb.	1.30pm to 3.59pm 1pm to 3.29pm 12.15pm to 2.44pm	4pm to 6.44pm 3.30pm to 6.14pm 2.45pm to 5.29pm	6.45pm to 9.29pm 6.15pm to 8.59pm 5.30pm to 8.14pm
PISCES	19 to end Feb. 1 to 10 Mar. 11 to 20 Mar.	11.30am to 1.59pm 11.15am to 1.44pm 10.30am to 12.59pm	2pm to 4.44pm 1.45pm to 4.29pm 1pm to 3.44pm	4.45pm to 7.29pm 4.30pm to 7.14pm 3.45pm to 6.29pm

	Birthdate	Libra	Scorpio	Sagittarius
ARIES	21 to 31 Mar. 1 to 10 Apr. 11 to 20 Apr.	5.30pm to 8.14pm 5pm to 7.44pm 4.15pm to 6.59pm	8.15pm to 10.59pm 7.45pm to 10.29pm 7pm to 9.44pm	11pm to 1.29am 10.30pm to 12.59am 9.45pm to 12.14am
TAURUS	21 to 30 Apr. 1 to 10 May 11 to 21 May	3.30pm to 6.14pm 3pm to 5.44pm 2.30pm to 5.14pm	6.15pm to 8.59pm 5.45pm to 8.29pm 5.15pm to 7.59pm	9pm to 11.29pm 8.30pm to 10.59pm 8pm to 10.29pm
GEMINI	22 to 31 May 1 to 10 Jun. 11 to 21 Jun.	2pm to 4.44pm 1.30pm to 4.14pm 12.45pm to 3.29pm	4.45pm to 7.29pm 4.15pm to 6.59pm 3.30pm to 6.14pm	7.30pm to 9.59pm 7pm to 9.29pm 6.15pm to 8.44pm
CANCER	22 to 30 Jun. 1 to 11 Jul. 12 to 22 Jul.	12pm to 2.44pm 11.30am to 2.14pm 11am to 1.44pm	2.45pm to 5.29pm 2.15pm to 4.59pm 1.45pm to 4.29pm	5.30pm to 7.59pm 5pm to 7.29pm 4.30pm to 6.59pm
LEO	23 to 31 Jul. 1 to 11 Aug. 12 to 23 Aug.	9.45am to 12.29pm 9.15am to 11.59am 8.30am to 11.14am	12.30pm to 3.14pm 12pm to 2.44pm 11.15am to 1.59pm	3.15pm to 5.44pm 2.45pm to 5.14pm 2pm to 4.29pm
VIRGO	24 to 31 Aug. 1 to 11 Sep. 12 to 22 Sep.	7.30am to 10.14am 7am to 9.44am 6.15am to 8.59am	10.15am to 12.59pm 9.45am to 12.29pm 9am to 11.14am	1pm to 3.29pm 12.30pm to 2.59pm 11.45am to 2.14pm
LIBRA	23 to 30 Sep. 1 to 11 Oct. 12 to 23 Oct.	5.10am to 8.14am 5am to 7.44am 4.15am to 6.59am	8.15am to 10.59am 7.45am to 10.29am 7am to 9.44am	11am to 1.29pm 10.30am to 12.59pm 9.45am to 12.14pm
SCORPIO	24 to 31 Oct. 1 to 11 Nov. 12 to 22 Nov.	3.30am to 6.14am 2.45am to 5.29am 2.15am to 4.59am	6.15am to 8.59am 5.30am to 8.14am 5am to 7.44am	9am to 11.29am 8.15am to 10.44am 7.45am to 10.14am
SAGITTARIUS	23 to 30 Nov 1 to 11 Dec. 12 to 21 Dec.	1.30am to 4.14am 12.45am to 3.29am 12.15am to 2.59am	4.15am to 6.59am 3.30am to 6.14am 3am to 5.44am	7am to 9.29am 6.15am to 8.44am 5.45am to 8.14am
CAPRICORN	22 to 31 Dec. 1 to 11 Jan. 12 to 20 Jan.	11.15pm to 1.59am 10.45pm to 1.29am 10.15pm to 12.59am	2am to 4.44am 1.30am to 4.14am 1am to 3.44am	4.45am to 7.14am 4.15am to 6.44am 3.45am to 6.14am
AQUARIUS	21 to 31 Jan. 1 to 10 Feb. 11 to 18 Feb.	9.30pm to 12.14am 9pm to 11.44pm 8.15pm to 10.59pm	12.15am to 2.59am 11.45pm to 2.29am 11pm to 1.44am	3am to 5.29am 2.30am to 4.59am 1.45am to 4.14am
PISCES	19 to end Feb. 1 to 10 Mar. 11 to 20 Mar.	7.30pm to 10.14pm 7.15pm to 9.59pm 6.30pm to 9.14pm	10.15pm to 12.59am 10pm to 12.44am 9.15pm to 11.59pm	1am to 3.29am 12.45am to 3.14am 12am to 2.29am

	Birthdate	Capricorn	Aquarius	Pisces
ARIES	21 to 31 Mar. 1 to 10 Apr. 11 to 20 Apr.	1.30am to 3.14am 1am to 2.44am 12.15am to 1.59am	3.15am to 4.29am 2.45am to 3.59am 2am to 3.14am	4.30am to 5.29am 4am to 4.59am 3.15am to 4.14am
TAURUS	21 to 30 Apr. 1 to 10 May 11 to 21 May	11.30pm to 1.14am 11pm to 12.44am 10.30pm to 12.14am	1.15am to 2.29am 12.45am to 1.59am 12.15am to 1.29am	2.30am to 3.29am 2am to 2.59am 1.30am to 2.29am
GEMINI	22 to 31 May 1 to 10 Jun. 11 to 21 Jun.	10pm to 11.44pm 9.30pm to 11.14pm 8.45pm to 10.29pm	11.45pm to 12.59am 11.15pm to 12.29am 10.30pm to 11.44pm	1am to 1.59am 12.30am to 1.29am 11.45pm to 12.44am
CANCER	22 to 30 Jun. 1 to 11 Jul. 12 to 22 Jul.	8pm to 9.44pm 7.30pm to 9.14pm 7pm to 8.44pm	9.45pm to 10.59pm 9.15pm to 10.29pm 8.45pm to 9.59pm	11pm to 11.59pm 10.30pm to 11.29pm 10pm to 10.59pm
LEO	23 to 31 Jul. 1 to 11 Aug. 12 to 23 Aug.	5.45pm to 7.29pm 5.15pm to 6.59pm 4.30pm to 6.14pm	7.30pm to 8.44pm 7pm to 8.14pm 6.15pm to 7.29pm	8.45pm to 9.44pm 8.15pm to 9.14pm 7.30pm to 8.29pm
VIRGO	24 to 31 Aug. 1 to 11 Sep. 12 to 22 Sep.	3.30pm to 5.14pm 3pm to 4.44pm 2.15pm to 3.59pm	5.15pm to 6.29pm 4.45pm to 5.59pm 4pm to 5.14pm	6.30pm to 7.29pm 6pm to 6.59pm 5.15pm to 6.14pm
LIBRA	23 to 30 Sep. 1 to 11 Oct. 12 to 23 Oct.	1.30pm to 3.14pm 1pm to 2.44pm 12.15pm to 1.59pm	3.15pm to 4.29pm 2.45pm to 3.59pm 2pm to 3.14pm	4.30pm to 5.29pm 4pm to 4.59pm 3.15pm to 4.14pm
SCORPIO	24 to 31 Oct. 1 to 11 Nov. 12 to 22 Nov.	11.30am to 1.14pm 10.45am to 12.29pm 10.15am to 11.59am	1.15pm to 2.29pm 12.30pm to 1.44pm 12pm to 1.14pm	2.30pm to 3.29pm 1.45pm to 2.44pm 1.15pm to 2.14pm
SAGITTARIUS	23 to 30 Nov. 1 to 11 Dec. 12 to 21 Dec.	9.30am to 11.14am 8.45am to 10.29am 8.15am to 9.59am	11.15am to 12.29pm 10.30am to 11.44am 10am to 11.14am	12.30pm to 1.29pm 11.45am to 12.44pm 11.15am to 12.14pm
CAPRICORN	22 to 31 Dec. 1 to 11 Jan. 12 to 20 Jan.	7.15am to 8.59am 6.45am to 8.29am 6.15am to 7.59am	9am to 10.14am 8.30am to 9.44am 8am to 9.14am	10.15am to 11.14am 9.45am to 10.44am 9.15am to 10.14am
AQUARIUS	21 to 31 Jan. 1 to 10 Feb. 11 to 18 Feb.	5.30am to 7.14am 5am to 6.44am 4.15am to 5.59am	7.15am to 8.29am 6.45am to 7.59am 6am to 7.14am	8.30am to 9.29am 8am to 8.59am 7.15am to 8.14am
PISCES	19 to end Feb. 1 to 10 Mar. 11 to 20 Mar.	3.30am to 5.14am 3.15am to 4.59am 2.30am to 4.14am	5.15am to 6.29am 5am to 6.14am 4.15am to 5.29am	6.30am to 7.29am 6.15am to 7.14am 5.30am to 6.29am

Here is an example using this method:

Stuart Fenton was born at 8.35 p.m. BST on 31 July 1968. Deduct one hour to make the revised birth time 7.35 p.m. GMT 31 July is in the first (uppermost) section of the three Leo dates. The last but one column shows a birth time of 7.30 p.m. to 8.44 p.m. The column is headed 'Aquarius', therefore Stuart has the sign of Aquarius on the ascendant. Furthermore, we can see that he only just comes inside the limits of this birth time which gives him an early degree of Aquarius rising. An accurate computer reading which took into account the exact place of birth as well as the time of birth confirmed that Stuart's actual ascendant is 5° Aquarius.

Quick method for births elsewhere in the northern hemisphere

This quick method becomes less accurate the further away from Greenwich the birth occurs, so I do suggest that you take your data to an astrologer. However, in the meantime, you can adjust the time of birth as follows:

GMT (used throughout all astrology books)	0 hours
Eastern standard time 75° west	add 5 hours
Central standard time 90° west	add 6 hours
Mountain standard time 105° west	add 7 hours
Pacific standard time 120° west	add 8 hours
Yukon standard time 135° west	add 9 hours
Alaska/Hawaii standard time 150° west	add 10 hours
Bering time 165° west	add 11 hours

For births in the eastern hemisphere, reverse the procedure and *deduct* hours as required.

This method is too generalized for the southern hemisphere.

Home computer calculations

If you own a personal computer and don't mind spending a bit of money on an astrological programme, you can contact one of the software houses which advertise in astrological magazines. A simple programme which will give you enough information to make up natal and progressed charts will actually cost less than visiting an astrologer and having a full chart interpretation!

Calculating your ascendant by hand

It is worth noting here that astrology is a creative and interpretive skill which suits the slightly arty or linguistic type of person, therefore the person who makes a good natural astrologer is usually a poor mathematician. I am an absolute dunce where maths are concerned, yet I can calculate an ascendant, which goes to show that anyone can.

Here is an example of someone who was born in London (Great Britain) at 02.18 (2.18 a.m.) on the 21 August 1965. The subject's name is Helen. (NB: I have used a *midnight* ephemeris for these calculations.)

1. As Helen was born in London, there is no need to make any adjustment for place of birth. Astrological calculations are based on the proximity of the birth to the Greenwich meridian.

   02.18.00
   1.00.00 −
   ⸻
2. An August birth means that British Summer Time was in operation, therefore deduct one hour making the birth time 01.18 GMT.

   01.18.00
   ⸻
3. The sidereal time (exact star time rather than calendar time) at midnight on 21 August was 21 hours 56 minutes 25 seconds.

   21.56.25
4. Add the time of birth to the sidereal time. Remember that when adding there are 60 seconds to a minute and 60 minutes to an hour.

   21.56.25
   1.18.00 +
   ⸻
   23.14.25
   ⸻
5. Now you will have to make an extra calculation which is called 'interval time'. This means that you add 10 seconds for every hour, 5 for every half hour or 3 for every 20 minutes. If you forget this, the chart will be slightly inaccurate but not by so much that the actual rising sign will be changed

   23.14.25
   13 +
   ⸻
   23.14.38
   ⸻
6. Now look up the resulting figures in an

ephemeris (book of ascendants and planetary   23.14.38
positions).

7. In Helen's case, when we look in the   23.12.10
   ephemeris, we can see that her figure of   =17°37'
   23hrs 14mins 38secs falls between 23.12.10
   which comes out as 17° 37' of Cancer and
   23.15.52 which comes out as 18° 20' of   23.15.52
   Cancer. For most purposes the round figure   =18°20'
   of 18° of Cancer which falls between the two ***23.14.38
   will be quite good enough.   =Approx. 18°

In order to double check this I ran the co-ordinates through my
computer, even taking account of the fact that Helen's actual
place of birth was 11 minutes of a degree to the west of
Greenwich. The computer gave an exact reading of 17° 57' of
Cancer. As there are 60 minutes in every degree, the figure of
17° 57' is as near as dammit 18° Cancer.

This kind of calculation will do for births in the southern part
of Great Britain. For births in the north, follow exactly the same
procedure but look at the figures for Liverpool rather than for
London in a table of houses or in your ephemeris.

The nit-picker's guide to a fully calculated ascendant
Example: James Smith. Born in New York City at 2.15 p.m.
(14.15) on 10 January 1968.

1. Check that the date is correct because Americans sometimes
   reverse the day and the month so that 10.7.68 could be 7
   October 1968!
2. Check for daylight saving. If you are going to do much of this
   kind of work, you will need a couple of books which are
   called *Time Changes in the World* and *Time Changes in the
   USA*. These can be obtained from specialist dealers.
3. Look up the map reference for New York City.

Revision section
Date: 10.7.68
Daylight saving: Yes, one hour.
Map Refs: 40°45' North, 74°0' West.

Calculations

1.	Note down the birth time in hours, minutes and seconds.	14.15.00
2.	Deduct 1 hour for daylight saving.	14.15.00 1.00.00 − ———— 13.15.00
3.	Convert the local mean time to GMT. New York uses a time zone which is 5 hours behind Greenwich, therefore add 5 hours.	13.15.00 5.00.00 + ———— 18.15.00
4.	Look up the sidereal time in a midnight ephemeris for midnight (00.00) on 10.7.68.	19.11.55
5.	Add the birth time to the sidereal time	19.11.55 18.15.00 + ———— 37.26.55
6.	Add 10 seconds for every hour which has been added, also 5 seconds for every half hour.	37.26.55 3.02 + ———— 37.29.57
7.	Deduct the exact longitude from the new time. New York is 74° west of Greenwich, therefore the exact difference is 4 hours 56 minutes. This is based on 4 minutes for every degree of longitude.	37.29.57 4.56.00 − ———— 32.33.57

8.	The tables of houses are based on figures from 0 to 24 hours. Our sample figure is more than 24 hours; therefore we must deduct 24 hours and look up the resulting figure in the tables.	32.33.57 24.00.00 − ———— 8.33.57 ————
9.	A book called *Raphaels Tables of Houses for Northern Latitudes* (or something which does the same thing) will be needed for this part of the calculation.	

In my Raphael's Tables, the nearest figure to our result of 8.33.57 is 8.33.35. This few seconds difference is negligible, therefore we may safely conclude that James has an ascendant of 0°20′ Scorpio and a mid-heaven of 6° Leo.

Further complications

If James had been born at exactly the same map references but *south* of the equator, he would have first seen the light of day at a place in Chile called the Archipelago de los Chonos. If that were the case, we would have to work out the calculations up to the end of step 8 and then *add* 12 hours. After looking up the ascendant and mid-heaven, we would then need to *reverse* the resulting ascendant and mid-heaven to give us the new southern latitude ascendant of 28°46′ Scorpio and a mid-heaven of 6° Leo.

All professional astrologers are familiar with this routine and, when exactitude is required, they will also fine tune the map references and correctly locate the planets for time of birth by means of logarithms. Computers reduce what was once a day's work calculating a chart into the work of a few minutes and they do it with perfect accuracy. But even when using a computer, remember to adjust the time differential – e.g. deduct any daylight saving and add or subtract to bring the time to GMT.

CHAPTER 3

How the Signs of the Zodiac are Arranged

The signs of the zodiac are always listed in the following order.

1. Aries
2. Taurus
3. Gemini
4. Cancer
5. Leo
6. Virgo
7. Libra
8. Scorpio
9. Sagittarius
10. Capricorn
11. Aquarius
12. Pisces

The signs with odd numbers (Aries, Gemini, Leo, Libra, Sagittarius and Aquarius) are masculine/positive in character. This suggests extroversion, confidence and assertiveness, and the ability to solve problems with courage and enterprise. The even numbered signs (Taurus, Cancer, Virgo, Scorpio, Capricorn and Pisces) are feminine/negative in character. These suggest introversion, shyness and passivity, the ability to nurture, conserve and to solve problems by intuitive means.

The signs are grouped into ancient elements of fire, earth, air and water:

The fire signs are Aries, Leo and Sagittarius.
The earth signs are Taurus, Virgo and Capricorn.
The air signs are Gemini, Libra and Aquarius.
The water signs are Cancer, Scorpio and Pisces.

The signs are also grouped into the ancient qualities of cardinal, fixed and mutable:

The cardinal signs are Aries, Cancer, Libra and Capricorn.
The fixed signs are Taurus, Leo, Scorpio and Aquarius.
The mutable signs are Gemini, Virgo, Sagittarius and Pisces.

The fire signs – Aries, Leo, Sagittarius

The key ideas here are of energy, enthusiasm and optimism. These people need to be in the centre of whatever is going on, thoroughly involved and even directing. Fire people take the initiative and throw their enthusiasm, intuition and faith behind any enterprise. They never quite relinquish their childhood and are therefore very much in tune with young people and young ideas.

Fire people are egotistic, headstrong and sometimes arrogant but they are also generous, warm-hearted and spontaneously kind, preferring to help others wherever possible than to take advantage of them. Fire people get things started; they create activity but need a back-up team to fill in the details for them. These people are quick to grasp an idea and tackle it with gusto, treating life like a kind of game, complete with the sportsman's sense of fair play. They find it impossible to save for a rainy day but will invariably find a way to earn money when in trouble. Oddly enough fire people are often very materialistic, measuring their self-worth by their ability to accumulate money and posessions and by having an expensive lifestyle. These people are quick to anger but rarely sulk.

Fire rising

When a fire sign is on the ascendant, the outer manner is friendly, uncritical and non-hostile which makes these people good mixers and excellent public relations executives. Aries rising gives a well-organized, slightly military bearing which makes them fit well into any kind of para-military or civil service organization. Leo rising subjects have a dignified and rather formal manner which inspires confidence, while Sagittarius risers have a cheerful, pleasant and rather witty outer manner which suits all kinds of teaching, training and public speaking situations. The typically friendly but professionally competent signals which fire rising subjects send out draws a friendly and often rather respectful response from others.

The earth signs – Taurus, Virgo, Capricorn

The key ideas here are of practicality and security. Earth is concerned with structure and slow growth and also conventional behaviour and concrete results. This element is connected with physical things which can be touched and held and which perform a function. Earth people are sensible, they take their time over everything and tend to finish every task which they start. They are shrewd and careful, usually very good at figure work and also surprisingly dexterous so they don't often drop or break anything.

Earth people hate to waste anything and they are careful with their money. However they are invariably generous to their own families. They need a secure home and a solid financial base; requirements which make them appear materialistic to others. Earthy types like to socialize among small groups of familiar people who appreciate their intelligence and dry sense of humour. They may lack spontaneity and can be too cautious and fussy at times but they are reliable and capable. It takes time to get to know these individuals as they prefer to hang back in social situations, while in business situations they behave in a rather formal manner. Earth people are suspicious of the motives of others and are extra sensitive to hurt. They are slow to fall in love but when they do, they will remain loyal and faithful to their partner in the majority of cases.

Earth rising
When an earth sign is on the ascendant the outer manner is shy, serious and cautious. Taurus risers are the most sociable of the three and are often musical or artistic. Virgo risers look for mental stimulation in others while Capricorn risers enjoy both work and social pursuits. People with these signs on the ascendant send out signals which are pleasant and tactful suggesting they they prefer to form part of a team – at least to begin with – than to push themselves immediately to the front.

The air signs – Gemini, Libra, Aquarius

The key idea here is of communication. Air people are concerned with ideas and theories of all kinds including education, networks and news. They seek answers to questions and then go on to enlighten other people. The network of their nervous system is always on the alert and sometimes over-stretched. These people may be serious-minded intellectuals who are highly involved with the education system or the media, or they may be chirpy happy-go-lucky types who pick up their street-wise knowledge from the tabloid newspapers and the local pub. They can be found arguing, exploring ideas and becoming excited by means and methods which can apply to anything from the way the universe was formed to a recent football game. They make good journalists, shopkeepers, teachers and travellers because they are always up-to-date.

Although kind hearted and genuinely concerned with humanity, they can forget their many friends when they are out of sight. They cannot deal with emotional dependency on the part of others, as this drains them, leaving them exhausted and irritable. Air rising subjects love gadgets, especially those which help them communicate or travel, such as computers, fancy telephones and a good fast car.

Air rising

When an air sign is on the ascendant the subject is friendly and sociable but also independent and somewhat detached. The Gemini riser is constantly busy, fully engaged in a kind of juggling act with at least a dozen balls being kept in the air by some kind of mental sleight of hand. The Libra riser occupies himself with business schemes which often need the aid of a more earthy partner to make them come into fruition. The Aquarian riser makes wonderful plans for himself and for others and may even carry some of them out. Air risers can sometimes appear arrogant and offensive if threatened or caught off guard but they will rush to the aid of anyone who is genuinely in need. They send out rather superior, macho or businesslike signals which command the respect of others.

The water signs – Cancer, Scorpio, Pisces

The key ideas here are of emotion, intuition and feeling. These people may spend their lives helping others or at least involving themselves in human problems. They are attached to the kind of matters which bring beginnings, endings and transformations to the lives of others. Watery people respond slowly when asked a question and may appear slow to grasp a new concept but this is deceptive because they are filtering the ideas through their layers of intuition before accepting them. Being slow to change, they prefer familiar surroundings and the closeness of family and friends.

Water people are often quite tense and can worry themselves into illness. They need a lot of understanding as their moods and emotions make them changeable and unfathomable at times. They are the kindest of friends, often giving practical and sensible help when it is needed but they cannot take too much neurotic dependence from others. These people are hypersensitive, creative and often psychic. They can appear withdrawn and distant in some cases but they desperately need stable relationships with plenty of love and affection.

Water rising

When a water sign is on the ascendant the subject will hide his true feelings. He fears the world around him and feels a strong need to protect himself and also, in some cases, to protect the helpless. What you see is definitely *not* what you get with these people. Cancerians appear chatty and helpful and they do well in any situation which requires tact. Scorpio risers use many different forms of camouflage, one of their favourites being offensiveness and an off-putting manner. It is always worth being patient with such people because there is often a reason for their difficult attitude and the reward is usually worth the effort. Pisces risers appear soft, gentle, self-sacrificing and sometimes even helpless but don't be taken in, they will fight strongly and sometimes underhandedly for what they think is right. The signals which these types give out are consciously or subconsciously chosen for their effect, making them appear fierce, friendly, peaceful or docile depending upon their choice of mask.

Cardinal

Cardinal people cannot be held under anyone's thumb, they need to take charge of their own world. Their energies may be directed towards themselves, their homes and families or to the wider world of work and politics. The cardinal signs, being on the angles of a birthchart, provide the energy and initiative to get things moving.

Fixed

Fixed people have the strength and endurance to see things through and to uphold the status quo. They rarely change their homes, careers or partnerships, preferring to live with an existing situation rather than face uncertainty. Fixed people are loyal and dependable but also very obstinate. They project an image of strength which is an effective shield for their considerable vulnerability.

Mutable

These people can adapt to the prevailing circumstances at any given time while, at the same time, managing to alter a situation to suit themselves. Mutable people can steer projects through periods of transition as well as, when necessary, bringing things to a conclusion. Although gentle and likable, mutable people can be quite ruthless when the need arises.

PART TWO
Rising Sign-by-Sign

CHAPTER 4

Aries Rising

The whole art of war consists of getting
at what is on the other side of the hill.

Arthur Wellesley, 1st Duke of
Wellington

A few words of explanation

A sign on the ascendant expresses itself in a different way from a
Sun sign. However, some of the characteristics, if only the
childhood experiences, will apply if you have the Sun in Aries or
in the first house. They may be present if you have Mars in Aries
or in the first house; if your Moon is in Aries your emotions and
reactions will have an Arian flavour. If the ascendant is weak
(see Chapter 1), the Aries overlay will not be so noticeable. If

the rest of the birthchart is very different from the rising sign, there could be a conflict in the personality. This is because the outer manner, as displayed by the signals which are given out on first meeting the subject, is different from the main character which lies underneath. However, Aries is so direct and open that this is far less likely to be the case than with some of the other ascendants. Another possibility is that the subject rejects all that his parents, parent figures and teachers stood for, and creates a life for himself which is very different from the one which they envisaged for him, or from the one he lived through as a child.

Remember that this sign is cardinal which implies the start of anything, and also a fire sign which implies enthusiasm and impulsiveness. It is masculine/positive in its approach which suggests an outwardly extrovert nature. Aries rising is a sign of *short ascension* which means that it only applies in the northern hemisphere for a very short period of time in any day – therefore only a few British people are born each day with this sign on the ascendant.

Early experiences
If you are one of these rare creatures, the chances are that there was something missing in your childhood. Many Aries rising children are born into military families who move about from one place to another. They may also spend a part of each year at boarding school. The child experiences feelings of strangeness, dislocation and of distance from the parents. Self-reliance and some measure of self-centredness are natural for Aries risers, even if their childhood experiences don't force this upon them, and this can make it difficult for them to form successful family relationships later on.

The Aries riser may opt for a life in the services where he becomes part of a larger family-type group. Several years ago, I did a horoscope for a rather sturdy looking middle-aged lady who was coming to the end of a service career. She told me that it had been a good life full of travel and good fellowship, and that she wasn't quite sure what she was going to do with her time now that she was a civilian once more.

Aries risers who grow up in a normal, stay-at-home family

often experience discord and conflict. There may be a difficult relationship between the child and his parents; this is especially true of the father/son relationship. There can't be two bosses in one family and, in this case, neither wants to concede any kind of authority to the other. It is quite usual for the two to be very different in character with little real understanding between them, it seems that neither can really approve of the other and there could be some pretty noisy disagreements.

Paul, an Aries rising guy, cut himself off from his parents as soon as he grew up and has had as little as possible to do with them ever since. Diana, another Aries rising subject, had quite a good childhood but never became close to her father. Her older sister worshipped him and couldn't see any wrong in him (at least until much later in life) whereas Diana could see him warts and all and therefore experienced a far cooler relationship with him. It is worth remembering that an Arian nature makes for a noisy, bouncy and rather bumptious child whose restless behaviour and argumentative ways can aggravate even the most saintly of parents.

In some cases, the parents are sporty and adventurous by nature encouraging a kind of gung-ho bravery in the child. This is all very well if the child is also an outdoor and athletic type, but if he isn't the parents will write him off as an over-timid wimp. This situation is even more likely to work the other way around. One such example is Miriam who was brought up in a classically claustrophobic pre-war Jewish family where both her parents and her sister studiously avoided anything which might involve the slightest hint of danger. In addition to this, her mother coddled her younger sister. Miriam wasn't the kind to encourage coddling, being a raw-boned athletic type of child who ran up, climbed on and jumped off everything at the slightest opportunity. On those occasions when she found herself in real trouble, stuck up a tree, for example, her mother's reaction was to fall down in a faint. This, to Miriam's eyes, confirmed her opinion that her mother was useless and ineffective. Incidentally, Miriam is still leaping about now that she is in her eighties! Human nature being totally contrary, Miriam still feels that she was unnecessarily deprived of the love and approval of her parents.

Women who have this rising sign have a masculine outlook on life, which may lead them to experience difficulty in adapting to the traditional feminine role. This does not imply that all Aries rising women are raving lesbians; on the contrary, these women get on very well with men, enjoying their company and sharing their interests. Some women prefer not to marry, either living an independent life with or without boyfriends or finding happiness within a military career. I imagine that the rather hearty kind of nun who enjoys fixing the convent's vehicles might be an Aries rising subject. Those who do marry and have a family need an interesting career outside the home in order to sop up their extra energy and give them something worthwhile to do. Fortunately, these days, there is plenty of scope for the extrovert, enthusiastic Aries woman to have the unrestricted independent kind of lifestyle that she needs.

It is worth remembering that the sign on the cusp of the fourth house (the IC) which is concerned with family matters is, in this case, Cancer. This makes you a surprisingly caring family member, even to the extent of being self-sacrificial in this area of your life, but more of this in the characteristics section later on.

When I take a look at Aries rising or even Sun in Aries subjects in reality rather than by blindly following the rules of astrology, I find a common theme. Many of you come from small families who themselves have little contact with their own relatives, either because your parents moved away from the area where their own relatives lived, or because they chose to cut themselves off from them. The Arian child, therefore, doesn't have the opportunity of benefiting from a wider family group and this leaves him with only his parents' views and values to fall back on. Frequently these values are distorted and lacking in common sense. Furthermore, the Arian child is often an only child, or so separated in age and type from the other siblings that he feels like an only child.

It is likely that one or both parents disliked you or saw no value in you. There was no discernible reason for this, you were simply viewed as an irritation or an inconvenience. This leads many of you to seek self-validation through marriage, often marrying young and choosing an older partner, or someone who is deemed to be wiser and more competent at the game of life. If the marriage doesn't work out, you may begin to philander. There is no guarantee that second or subsequent relationships work out either, unless you are able to go through a good deal of self-analysis and reach a stage where you can finally throw off the distorted lessons of your childhood.

Some Arians succeed in one-to-one relationships, but go on to face difficulties in relating to their children. The Arian never quite grows up enough to be able to cope with the role of parent and, therefore, either leans too far towards the position of authority and dominance, becoming a bully towards his own children, or overdoes the nurturing role by clinging to them and sacrificing on their behalf for far too long. It seems as if the 'pulling factor' at the top of the chart (Capricorn) leads to too much authority, while in other cases the 'pulling factor' at the bottom of the chart (Cancer) leads to too much clinging.

However, nothing stays the same forever; children grow up and relationships come and go. With a bit of luck you can learn from life and finally make some kind of viable relationship which brings you pleasure. Perhaps in compensation, Aries subjects often have a good friend or two, while others make a viable 'family' out of a couple of pet animals.

Basically this is neither the best nor the worst sign to have on the ascendant. There may have been loneliness in childhood but this seems to breed Arian self-reliance and doesn't usually cause you to have any difficulty in relating to others later on in life. Aries is a sociable sign and, on the whole, a cheerful and optimistic one.

Appearance
Bearing in mind racial differences, family tendencies and the influence of the rest of your birthchart, the Aries influence would suggest a shortish stature with a strong and muscular body (which may run to fat later); your arms and shoulders are strong and you can lift and carry surprisingly heavy weights for your size. Your face is broad across the eyes and maybe rounded

with a rather large head for your body. Arian eyes are neither protruding nor deep set, they stare out honestly from under thick, arched eyebrows. Aries rising women can do a lot with eye make-up as there is a rather large and flat area of eyelid to play with. The hair may be reddish in colour, quickly going grey. Men of this sign lean towards baldness – well, they do say that bald men are sexy! Women may moan about their thin and awkward hair which needs much perming and colouring in order to keep it looking good. Arians don't, as a rule, have much body hair.

Being a palmist as well as an astrologer, I tend to notice people's hands. Arian hands are small and graceful even in those cases when they are plump. The finger-nails have a characteristic 'A' shape, being much wider at the tip than at the cuticle end. These hands are used so elegantly that an Aries-type guy can quite mistakenly be taken as being gay! Most Arians walk quickly and move fast, they are graceful and light on their feet which may add to their slightly feminine appearance. Don't be taken in; these guys are far from being gay – though they might be very cheerful, especially when making love to an attractive woman.

Aries women are also graceful and are often good dancers. They too are unlikely to be gay despite the fact that their mental outlook is adventurously masculine. Their quick wit and ready smile, plus their somewhat childlike appearance is quite endearing to the opposite sex. To my mind, Jimmy Tarbuck has an Aries appearance, as does Mark McManus who plays Taggart in the TV series of that name.

Outer manner

You present yourself in a cheerful, friendly, non-hostile manner but may find it hard to conceal your contempt for those whose minds and actions are slower than your own. Not being easily influenced, you prefer to make up your own mind about everything, and you can appear rather opinionated. Others see you as quick, clever and courageous but they may become annoyed by your tendency to push yourself to the front of every queue and to fight for the best of whatever is going. Your sense of humour and child-like appeal can help you get away with murder – especially with the opposite sex.

Aries characteristics

This section can double up as a brief guide to Aries as a Sun sign *or* as a rising sign, so it makes a handy reference if you need to check out some Sun sign characteristics as well as those for the rising sign.

If yours is a strong rising sign, you will display a fair amount of Aries behaviour. You are probably the most capable and energetic person in your family, prepared to fight for their rights, and look after their interests, against all comers. Your career is important to you, and you use your earnings in order to give the members of your family what they need. Arians think, move and walk quickly; many enjoy speed for its own sake and cannot get by without owning a fast car. Being quick to take action and to throw your enthusiasm behind any venture, you sometimes step on the toes of slower more sensitive types. Being honest and frank, others always know where they stand with you, and on occasion you can be too honest for comfort because lies and prevarication don't come easily to you.

There is a tendency to argumentativeness; it might just be that you enjoy a stimulating debate but some of you will argue about anything. Your temper erupts quickly but usually settles down just as quickly, and thankfully, you don't sulk. Oddly enough, you prefer a rather structured life; you cannot cope with too much change except for those changes which you yourself initiate, neither can you take too much adversity. When too many pressures arise at once, your natural ebullience and confidence evaporate leaving you to fall back on other steadier members of the family for support. Some Aries rising subjects lash out when angry and either give whoever is in the way a verbal bashing or, worse still, a physical one.

There is a strange need for you to spoil yourself or to be spoiled by others. Perhaps this stems from your slightly neglected childhood. Arians love gadgetry; the current age of Japanese wizardry is just made for you. You may spend your money on expensive sports equipment which you never actually find the time or the patience to use properly. Certainly you will spend money on your hobbies whatever they may be, always making sure that you have the best equipment which can be bought. Some Arians spend money on household gadgets, abandoning them if they are found to be useless. A new car, boat, caravan or any other kind of vehicle is always an exciting buy.

You don't seek to deprive others in order to have the things you fancy, but male Arians may simply forget that their wives also need some spoiling. When you do buy something for your wife, it is something beautiful and very personal such as clothing, underwear or jewellery. Arian women love gold and jewellery, and both sexes love to have a wardrobe which is stuffed with the latest and nicest fashions.

You can be surprisingly snobbish and contemptuous of those whom you see as being inferior. You like your family to move in the right circles and for your children to become educated and accomplished in an almost Victorian manner. This seems to stem from a concealed contempt for your own background and an upwardly mobile desire to get away from all that it represented to you.

My friend and colleague, Eve Bingham, pointed out that many Arians have a talent for self-sacrifice, especially in respect of their family. She's right. I have seen Arians running around after their elderly parents to an extent which is above and beyond the call of duty. There are others who seem to give up most of their time and money to their children. There is some method in this particular form of madness, however, because what the Arian is after is *control*. By taking charge of the situation and making himself indispensable, he keeps the people concerned in a situation where he can keep an eye upon them.

The mid-heaven
This section and those which follow apply *only* to Aries rising and not to Sun in Aries. The mid-heaven can show the subject's aims and ambitions, his attitude to work and his public standing. An Aries rising child may not show much interest in learning while he is at school but, as he reaches his teens, his desire for money and status will lead him to work hard and make achievements. He may also return to study later on in order to gain some specific qualification.

All Aries rising subjects have the sign of Capricorn on their mid-heaven, which suggests that you work best in a well ordered structure, perhaps in a large public service organization. Some of you prefer to run your own well-planned businesses. You are determined and capable. Your leadership qualities and common sense attitude to money can lead to great success, but this could well come rather late in life. You prefer to start something new, but if you do take over an existing position or an existing team, you soon reorganize it to reflect your own personal style. You could be drawn to the Arian careers of engineering, public service or the armed services, or to the Capricornian ones of business and banking. Red tape gets you down, and you become irritated by details. Company politics bore you, however, the world of National or local politics may be very attractive to you as a career. Your brain is excellent and, if the rest of the chart backs this up, you could find a future in the academic world.

Many Arians seem to spend years coasting along in a job making no discernible effort to push themselves forward until circumstances demand that an effort be made. Others are far more interested in the money which the job brings in or the company politics or the social life which comes with the job, rather than taking a real interest in the job for its own sake.

Despite the fact that the MC is supposed to represent aims, ambitions etc. it can also show the type of person whom you find attractive. A Capricorn partner, or one with a strong Saturn on the chart will be in sympathy with your goals in life and could well make a very pleasant complementary person with whom to live.

The descendant
The opposite point to the ascendant is the descendant or, in other words, the cusp of the seventh house. Traditionally, this is supposed to show the kind of person to whom we are attracted. In the case of Aries rising, the descendant is in Libra and it is surprising how many people who have either Aries rising or an Arian Sun do marry Librans. If your ascendant is late in Aries, a good deal of the seventh house will lie in Scorpio, so there could be an attraction to Scorpio types too. To be honest, I don't think that either Aries/Libra or Aries/Scorpio make particularly

successful matches, but the Aries/Libra mix works well in more detached areas such as business partnerships or, possibly, a short-lived affair, while Aries/Scorpio is too explosive in any kind of situation to survive for long.

In the case of Aries/Libra, the fiery enthusiastic Aries would be attracted by the calm detachment of Libra, his pleasantness, good taste and desire for harmony and balance. Librans are often good looking and stylish, which is attractive to you, but Libra's tendency to drift towards an easy and comfortable life would bore you, while your Aries energy and occasional tantrums would cause the Libran to switch off and tune out.

If the Scorpio partner were one of the sexy variety (contrary to popular opinion, many Scorpios are not especially sexy), there would be a strong initial attraction, but both are self-centred and bad tempered, and both would want to be the top dog. It is worth bearing in mind that the Aries riser himself may behave in a Libran way by trying to create a peaceful and harmonious atmosphere in a relationship.

Love, sex and relating – regardless of the descendant

Your most attractive features are generosity, honesty, spontaneous kindness and a sense of humour. To be honest, as long as your partner is humorous, intelligent and tolerant of your daft behaviour, you will be happy and so will your partner. You need an independent partner who has work and interests of his or her own, or better still someone who doesn't need to be waited on hand and foot. However, you need them within phone-shot so that you can have your needs attended to immediately! Aries risers don't require a terribly domesticated partner, but you do need help in the house and with the children as you, yourself, are not especially domesticated or tidy.

Your partner must give you space, not only for your career but also for your hobbies and interests. You need to be able to take off from time to time, either on business trips or sporting holidays with a group of mates. Your partner must understand that there is a side of you that needs this kind of freedom, and that this doesn't constitute either a lack of loyalty or a dereliction of duty.

You love your children very deeply, and want the best for

them, going to great lengths to educate them. However, you should try not to dominate your children or to show impatience, especially if they seem slow, timid, introverted or clumsy. If you behave impatiently to this kind of child, he will freeze up which will make him even more awkward and withdrawn, and will subsequently deprive you of the special kind of warmth that you could derive from a loving parent/child relationship.

With your abundance of energy, sex is an obvious necessity. You don't mind taking the lead in bed, and will be quite inventive but you must guard against selfishness especially while you are young and inexperienced. An un-Arian application of patience and thoughtfulness here will pay off. However, your natural kindness and generosity in this, as in all things, should ensure that you give as much as you get, so to speak. Remember that your partner may well enjoy the occasional sexual marathon but not necessarily every day and twice on Sundays! Arians are quite greedy where sex is concerned and can't really get enough of a good thing. Even a slightly dodgy relationship will work for you if the sexual side is good. In some ways, you suit a moody, changeable partner who varies in his or her sexual needs and responses from one day to the next so that you can avoid your pet hate − boredom.

Health

Traditionally, Aries rules the head down as far as the upper jaw. So headaches, eyes, ears, sinuses and the upper teeth are trouble spots. Some Aries rising subjects have bad skin and continue to fight off acne well into adult life. You have neither the time nor the nature to give in to illness, but sudden fevers and accidents are possibilities. You can become quite severely ill at times, but will bounce back quickly because your level of resistance is generally high. You enjoy food and may be a drinker, therefore weight gain could present a problem later in life, but if you maintain your preference for an active life, you quickly use up the extra calories.

Your sixth house is Virgo, so please also look at the Virgo section on health on page 105.

CHAPTER 5
Taurus Rising

Shall I compare thee to a summer's day?
Thou art more lovely and more temperate:
Rough winds do shake the darling buds of May,
and summer's lease hath all too short a date.

William Shakespeare, *Sonnet*

A few words of explanation

A sign on the ascendant expresses itself in a different way from
the Sun sign; however, some of the characteristics, even the
childhood experiences, will apply if you have the Sun in Taurus
or in the second house. Some of these characteristics will be
apparent if you have Venus in Taurus or in the second house. If
your Moon is in Taurus, your emotions and reactions will have a
Taurean flavour. If the ascendant is weak (see Chapter 1), the

Taurus overlay will not be so noticeable. If the rest of your birthchart is very different from the rising sign there could be conflict in the personality. This is because the outer manner, the signals which are given out by the Taurus rising subject on first meeting, are very different from the main character which lies underneath. Another possibility is that the subject rejects all that his parents, parent figures and teachers stood for and creates a life for himself which is very different from the one which they envisaged for him, or from the one he lived through as a child.

Remember that this is a fixed sign which implies the ability to stay with a situation and see it through. It is also an earth sign which implies practicality and a certain rootedness and it is feminine/negative which suggests introversion. This is a sign of *short ascension* which means that it only applies in our northern latitude for a short period of time in any day, therefore only a few people are born each day with this ascendant. However, it is not quite such a short ascending sign as Pisces or Aries, so there are a few more of you around than there are of them.

Early experiences

The sign of Taurus suggests comfort, and this was certainly true of your childhood. All the earth signs place an emphasis on the need for material security and, in the case of any earth sign on the ascendant, the subject's parents may accumulate money and goods in reaction to their own experiences of childhood poverty. They probably had to work very hard in order to make a home and bring up children. By the time you came along, your parents may have got over the early struggles, or may have still been trying to get it all together. Either way, the message given to the Taurus rising child is one of the need for security, comfort and better still, wealth.

The old-fashioned virtues of a steady job, money in the bank and solid family life were programmed into you but it is also possible that the 'Victorian' values of crass materialism and the devil-take-the-hindmost could also have been pushed upon you. This is fine if you have the same kind of requirements elsewhere in your birthchart, but not so good if you have a gamut of planets in a completely different type of sign, such as

Aquarius. Another and far more serious problem is that, although you were taken care of materially, you may have suffered emotional deprivation.

When a rising sign is both earthy and fixed, there is a strong possibility that one or both of the parents behaved in an authoritarian manner. Approval may have been given and withheld in subtle ways making you slightly withdrawn and rather mulish in return. Another possibility is that your father was a slightly awesome figure and that you were closer to, and more comfortable with, your mother. However, there is much that is good about this rising sign, and one could do a lot worse than to be born with a Taurean ascendant.

Your parents' outlook was conservative and their behaviour expressed moderation, commonsense, practicality and kindness. You were encouraged to be kind, thoughtful and conscientious. In the unlikely event that you grew up in anything other than the nuclear family, this would have been because one of your parents died. You are unlikely to have witnessed open discord or divorce at first hand. Civilized, unexpressed discontent might have been the order of the day in your parent's household.

You may have grown up with parents who were wrapped up in one another leaving you emotionally stranded, the consequence being that you learned to demand nothing and to avoid, at all costs, bringing the familiar look of irritation to their faces. If you were lucky enough to find another relative or perhaps a person outside the family to whom you could relate, the situation would not have been quite so bad. You may have been at odds with a brother or sister, either envying them for being more successful and more acceptable to your parents than you were, or, on the other hand, despising them for being dull, incompetent and irritating. This situation would also have caused you to hide your real feelings, to become devious or to boil inwardly. Your rage, on those occasions when you could no longer control yourself, would have been towering, frightening and quite destructive. As you grew older, you managed to avoid scenes or 'tune out' unpleasantness and ignore it altogether. This could make you difficult to live with because rather than face facts you continue to conceal your feelings, either erupting in anger or retreating into a world of silent withdrawal which is incomprehensible to others.

Somewhere along the line you will have been affected by beauty in some form or another. Many Taureans love gardening, because they can enjoy both the scent and beauty of the flowers and the production of their other love, good things to eat. It is possible that your parents were farmers or landscape gardeners because there is a natural feeling for the land and all that it produces. The twin messages of conservatism and conservation would lead you, in any situation, to build rather than destroy and to continue rather than to end.

Your family may have been instrumental in introducing you to the world of music, dance or art. You have a natural appreciation of beauty and harmony which derives from your ruling planet Venus. I know one Taurus rising lady who grew up in a 'dancing' family. Everyone in the family danced, some being professional or semi-professional ballet dancers, chorus line hoofers or ballroom dancers. Although she was a rather plump young woman, she took up ballroom dancing and reached quite a high standard.

If your home life was stable and your parents loving, united and caring, the situation at school was a little different. You were not the kind of child to cause trouble at school; disruption and disobedience is hardly your way of doing things. However, unless the rest of the chart is very different, you were probably slow to catch on, especially in the years before adolescence. Bad behaviour would have been expressed as stubbornness and a kind of switching off from the people around you. If your parents and teachers accepted you as you were, your school life would have been pleasant, if rather unproductive. However, if they didn't, then you might have been made to feel as if you were worthless and a failure in everything which was demanded of you.

Taureans are not the most sporty of children; many are plump and all of them hate to feel cold, wet and uncomfortable. Neither you nor your parents could see any value in romping around on a muddy sports field, although a Sunday afternoon tramp across the field with a dog was quite another matter. Your natural talent and interests lay in the areas of art and music. Nowadays, these interests are fostered for both sexes, but in the days when boys had to be boys and self-expression was not on the curriculum, this could have caused some suffering.

Far better for a beleaguered boy was your natural talent for making and mending things, so you probably enjoyed working with natural substances such as wood or clay. One area which attracted you was home economics, catering and dietetics. I can remember a client of mine who, while training as a dietician during her teens, had to switch to a secretarial course because her family's circumstances changed and they could no longer afford to keep her in training. She retained her interest in cooking and still makes the best cakes for miles around.

Basically, if you have a strong Taurean rising sign, your childhood would have been a better experience than for many others, although school was probably something of a trial, especially during your younger years. Many Taurus rising subjects develop an interest in reading and go on to educate themselves later in life at their own pace.

Appearance

Bearing in mind racial differences, family tendencies and the influence of the rest of your birthchart, the Taurean influence displays itself in a plump and sturdy body with a squarish head on a thick short neck. Taurean women look luscious when young but have to guard against weight gain later in life. Your complexion is clear, your eyes are marvellous and in white races your skin is rather pale and luminous. Your hands and feet are probably small. Your pleasant smile and gentle manner add to your attractive looks and take most people's minds off the fact that you might be a few pounds overweight. Oddly enough many Taurean types seem to like to hide their faces in some way. Men hide behind heavy rimmed glasses and beards, while women tend to wear plenty of make-up and have long wavy hair. It is fairly common for members of this rising sign to have a 'Churchillian' appearance.

Outer manner

Your outer manner is pleasant, slightly reserved but friendly and non-hostile. You enjoy a chat with neighbours or colleagues from the office, you probably enjoy listening to office gossip and jokes. Taureans, whether Sun sign or rising sign, have a good clean sense of humour which doesn't depend upon cruelty or sarcasm for effect. You appear slow moving to others, preferring to make your way through life at quite a gentle pace. Some Taureans give an appearance of hardness, especially in business situations but this is a form of protection and a cover-up.

Taurus characteristics

This section can double up as a brief guide to Taurus as a Sun sign *or* as a rising sign, so it makes a handy reference for you if you need to check out some Sun sign characteristics as well as the ones for the rising sign.

Conventional and sociable, you are pleasant companions and easy-going work-mates, as long as things are going your way! You don't like breaking promises, betraying a trust or leaving obligations unfulfilled. You are an exemplary employee, needing to feel as if you belong in a job, that your work is serving a useful purpose and that people are pleased with what you do. Work for work's sake doesn't excite you, but if temporarily short of cash, you'll cope with even the most boring job. You are capable and thorough, especially when left to do things at your own pace. While still on the subject of work, Taureans like concrete results, a nicely balanced set of figures or well filled shelves of stock. You can make and mend most things and can see the value of other people's work and make it useable and saleable. There will be more about career matters in the mid-heaven section later on in this chapter.

When coupled with someone who has a creative imagination, your ability to work with materials and make something concrete out of them is exceptional. My friend, Barry Gillam, who is a double Taurus (Sun and ascendant) lives with my pal, Kay Bielecki, a Leo. Although having very little money to play with, they bought a run-down house and gradually renovated it; they now have an attractive and comfortable home which has some intriguing and rather beautiful touches. Barry is typically Taurean in his ability to build and also to create a garden. All his work is carefully and properly prepared and finished; nothing slap-dash is good enough for him. Incidentally, most Taureans prefer to live in the country rather than in town.

You have the ability to finish all that you start and you rarely become rattled or walk away from a job if it doesn't go right straight away. You have patience with children and also with animals; indeed family life on a farm would probably suit you very well. You are in tune with nature even to the point of being interested in earth magic and the 'Craft'. (The Craft being Wicca or the ancient religion of white witchcraft.)

As a parent, you are patient and kind but you won't stand rudeness and bad behaviour. You seek a conventional education for your children and try to give them a practical and sensible upbringing. If they have any creative talent, you are happy to help them bring this out. There are times when your famous patience finally snaps and, on the odd occasion when you lose your temper, everyone around you runs for cover. Taureans are irritable when they are hungry. The worst time for your partner to tackle you on some thorny subject is the moment when you first put your foot in the front door after a hard day's work. After a meal and a rest, your temper is much improved, as is your sense of perspective.

The one characteristic which is guaranteed to be present when Taurus is the Sun sign or the rising sign, is the famous Taurean stubbornness and obstinacy. All the earth signs are happier with stability and are slow to change their minds and their lifestyles. Fixed sign people stand by their beliefs and principles and don't easily change their minds. Taurus is fixed earth, therefore the most reliable and the least flexible of all signs. I have one Taurus rising friend who appears to display very few Taurean characteristics, but when he received a tactless and somewhat insulting letter from a junior colleague, he merely compressed his mouth in a white-lipped smile. The junior's career came to a grinding halt from that time on.

Taureans traditionally are loyal, dependable and faithful in any relationship. If you became so unhappy with a partner, or so smitten with someone else that you are forced to leave, you would be just as loyal and faithful to the second partner as you had tried to be with the first. You prefer a stable relationship to courtship and you enjoy settling down to become part of a family. Many Taureans are so dedicated to relating that they put their partner even before their children. Your worst fault is a kind of emotional idleness. It is all too easy, when you are at home, to sit slumped in an armchair snoozing in front of the telly, taking your partner for granted to the point where you even forget to talk. Remember that a few outings and entertainments won't go amiss and this kind of thoughtfulness would be much appreciated by the other half! If you refuse to make any effort, you are in danger of waking up one day to find a note on the mantelpiece and a vacant space where the partner should be.

People of this sign have a totally unjustified reputation for being mean, materialistic and money-minded. It's true that you won't go out of your way to take on the problems of people outside of your immediate family, but this has something to do with your lack of spontaneity. It takes a certain kind of initiative to solve the world's problems and this is not a particularly Taurean feature. You don't throw money away if you can help it. You fear insolvency and you hate waste but you are not particularly mean, or at least, no more so than other 'careful' signs such as Cancer, Pisces or Capricorn.

The mid-heaven

This section and those which follow apply only to Taurus rising, *not* to Sun in Taurus. The mid-heaven shows the subject's aims and ambitions, his public standing and his attitude to work outside the home. In the case of births in the UK and in similar (northern) latitudes, the Taurus rising subject's mid-heaven is always in Capricorn. In much of the United States, people who have a late degree of Taurus on the ascendant may have Aquarius on the MC.

Taurus/Capricorn

Capricorn, like Taurus, is an earth sign but it is cardinal in nature, whereas Taurus is fixed. This cardinality on the MC may be one of the reasons why so many Taurus risers go in for running their own show, by owning their own businesses. Being an earth sign, you would tend to produce or supply goods which are practical and useful. You may run a shop, a gardening service, something in the farming or farm-supply line or a small factory. Many of you work in the building trade. Your love of beauty and your subtle sense of touch could lead you into the fields of dressmaking, cooking and craft-work. Some Taureans take up beauty therapy or become involved with the cosmetic industry, possibly as make-up artists. Many others find their way into the entertainment world, often as singers. However, life being what it is, many Taurus rising people actually work in offices and banks.

The Capricorn connection gives a fondness for big business and banking while the Taurean thoroughness ensures that errors are few.

Taurus/Aquarius
Generally speaking, Taurus rising subjects resist pressure and dislike hectic or worrying jobs but the Taurus/Aquarius combination is a little more able to cope with this. Remember that these are both fixed signs which need to do things at their own pace and in their own way. The ingenuity of Aquarius could produce a powerfully competent wheeler-dealer or someone who reaches the top in an unusual career. I guess that the combination of these two could produce a show-business impressario or the owner of a respected art auctioneering business. This combination adds determination and stubborn-ness.

Despite the fact that the mid-heaven is supposed to represent one's direction in life, it can also show the type of person who might attract you, especially if you require a partner who is in sympathy with your goals. Therefore, a partner who has a strong Capricorn or Aquarius emphasis on the chart could appeal to you.

The descendant
The opposite point to the ascendant is the descendant. This is traditionally supposed to show the type of person to whom we are initially attracted. In this case, the descendant is in

Scorpio; therefore a strong, equally dependable and almost equally stubborn partner is suggested. You seem to be looking for the fireworks which accompany the Scorpion, either in the form of uncertain moods or sexual energy.

I have no evidence of a particularly high incidence of Taurus/Scorpio relationships but I guess that this combination would work quite well. Both partners need stability in relationships, both are happier in familiar surroundings than with a life of constant change, both are dutiful family members who are also orientated towards getting on in life. There is much in common, but there are times when Scorpio's moods might be hard for Taurus to take. Both signs prefer commitment to playing the field.

Love, sex and relationships – regardless of the descendant

You can cope with a financially independent partner or even one who is heavily involved with a career, just as long as the emotional security is there. You need the love which might have been missing during your childhood. You like to know where your partner is, also what they are doing; not because you distrust them but because you feel safer if there are no mysteries going on around you. You also like your partner to be around at mealtimes.

Your senses are very acute and you like to indulge them. Sex competes even with food for your attention! Taureans have a reputation for being delightful lovers and a couple of female acquaintances of mine who live with Taurus rising men, tell me that they are very well looked after in bed! You know the expression 'enough is as good as a feast', don't you? Well, there's nothing Taurus likes better than a feast. A spiteful person might suggest that the Taurean propensity for being lazy means that you enjoy nothing better than a day spent in good company wrapped in a duvet wearing nothing but a smile.

On a more serious note, what Taurus rising subject's like best and need most is cuddling. The adult Taurus rising subject may still suffer the residual effects of the childhood lack of closeness between himself and his parents. This could give him a need to make up for lost comforts by way of touch and closeness in a relationship.

Health

Taurus is a robust sign with good powers of recovery. The weak spots are the throat, thyroid gland and the lower teeth. Weight may cause problems and the connection with the planet Venus might bring ailments such as cystitis and diabetes later in life.

Your sixth house is in Libra, so please also look at the health section on page 115.

CHAPTER 6
Gemini Rising

The flower that smiles today
Tomorrow dies:
All that we wish to stay
Tempts and then flies.
What is this world's delight?
Lightening that mocks the night.
Brief even as bright.

   Percy Bysshe Shelley, *Mutability*

A few words of explanation
A sign on the ascendant expresses itself in a different way from a
Sun sign. However, some of the characteristics, even the
childhood experiences, will apply if you have the Sun in Gemini
or in the third house. They may be present if you have Mercury

in Gemini or the third house and, if you have the Moon in Gemini or in the third house, your emotions and reactions will have a Gemini flavour. If the ascendant is weak (see Chapter 1), the Gemini overlay will not be noticeable. If the rest of your birthchart is very different from the rising sign there could be a conflict in the personality. This is because the outer manner and the signals which are given out when one first meets someone new are very different from the main character which lies underneath. The subject may reject all that his parents, teachers and parent figures stood for and go on to create a lifestyle for himself which is very different from the one which they envisaged for him or the one he experienced as a child.

Remember that this sign is mutable, which implies flexibility of mind. It is an air sign, which implies an intellectual approach to everything and it is masculine/positive which suggests an outwardly extrovert nature. Gemini rising is a sign of shortish to medium ascension, therefore there are fewer Gemini rising people born each day than there are of some of the other signs.

Early experiences

If you have this rising sign, your childhood may have been unsatisfactory, emotionally deprived or even something of a horror story. There may even have been a mystery surrounding your origins. If your childhood was genuinely all sweetness and light, I suggest that you actually re-check your birth time! I call this the 'orphan's ascendant' because there is a feeling of having been left out in the cold. A surprisingly high proportion of orphans, foundlings, fostered, adopted and Dr Barnardo's children seem to be born with Gemini on the ascendant. Many people who started out with two parents in the normal manner seem to mislay one or both of them somewhere along the way!

Even if you were brought up in a normal nuclear family, there would have been feelings of isolation and of being a square peg in a round hole. All this would have been bad enough for the silent withdrawn type who is given to hiding his feelings and putting on an act of dumb acceptance, but you're not like that, are you? You're friendly, garrulous and filled with a need to explain yourself to others. You need to communicate, to connect with other people on an intellectual level and to analyse yourself and the world around you in order to put it into a sensible and meaningful kind of order.

There may have been difficulty in your dealings with brothers and sisters; it is possible that you were brought up in some kind of patched-together family with older half-brothers and sisters or even cousins who became brothers and sisters of a kind to you. It is possible that yours was a large family in which you somehow missed out in the rush to gain your parent's attention. You may be so different from your natural parents and siblings that you appear to have originated from a different planet.

Tania, for example, was brought up in a normal nuclear family of mother, father, brother and two cats. The parents were kind and caring but wrapped up in each other and they were also burdened by commitments to elderly relatives. Both of Tania's parents worked hard to make a living, therefore the children were not able to take centre stage. Tania's older brother was a quiet studious kind of lad who developed an excellent relationship with his ascetic grandfather. Tania was bouncy, noisy, demanding, talkative and a trial to her sorely pressed parents. She spent a lot of time being overtly or subtly shoved out of the way, or snapped at for being a nuisance. There were not many opportunities for her to gain approval from anyone.

Tania now has a job in one of the caring professions; she travels a good deal and has many friends of her own. She is needed, respected for her work and approved of by those whom she helps. If this all sounds more like Pisces than Gemini, remember that these signs have much in common. Both are mutable signs and both have a strange kind of duality; the two fishes of Pisces and the Geminian twins are always tied together but often seem to be trying to travel in different directions.

You were probably one of the younger children or even actually the youngest child in the family, born to parents for whom the novelty of parenthood had rather worn off. You may have been pushed around or ignored by older siblings or left with minders, while your mother went out to earn much-needed extra money. Something may have gone badly wrong early in your childhood, maybe the death of a parent or some kind of financial disaster. You may have been acutely aware that the people with whom you had been left looked after you under sufferance or for money. Even in a more normal family, there is a feeling of being the odd one out.

You may have been an academic child in a practical family, or a school failure in a family where the only things which counted were brains and the exam papers. You may have had a personal or religious outlook which was different from that of the rest of the family. The whole thing may have been such a mess that, in the light of adult experience, the only thing to do is to put it all behind you, look at yourself as you are now and begin to build from there.

If your childhood was actually quite tolerable, you will have gained from the better side of this ascendant. The benefits are exposure to books, ideas and teaching aids of one kind or another from an early age. You were encouraged to read, write and to express yourself. If self-expression in the form of too much talking was discouraged, you will have been encouraged by your teachers to write, draw and make things. Being restless and lively, you enjoyed sports or dancing and you could have achieved a high standard. It is possible that you enjoyed being involved in some kind of youth organization but probably not for long as Geminians hate to be regimented. Even as an adult, you enjoy movement and often do most of your thinking while walking or exercising in the local swimming pool.

Gemini risers have an inventive streak and are often dexterous, so you can always find something with which to occupy yourself when there is nobody else around. This sign is not especially associated with animals, but you may like small animals which can be very comforting if your life is at all lonely. You may even talk to the goldfish, which is just one manifestation of your marvellous communications skills, but more of this in the mid-heaven section.

Gemini rising subjects are surprisingly ambitious and these ambitions may have seen the first light of day through childhood dreams. There is a feeling that, if you can develop some kind of strength, power or self-esteem, you can avoid being laughed at and shoved out of the way later in life. There are some among you who don't seem to learn the first time around and have to go through a sticky marriage before the message of your *apparent* worthlessness in the eyes of close family members finally reaches your brain.

Geminis are workers; this is your salvation. You probably have two or more careers going at once, together with a couple of committee positions to boot. You need to feel important and, one day, you realize with a jolt that you *are* important and no one talks down to you any more. The Gemini clown then disappears for ever, being replaced by the Gemini ring-master.

Appearance
Bearing in mind family and racial tendencies, plus the rest of the chart, you are likely to be shortish, slim and neat in appearance. You prefer to wear your hair in a short and tidy style, partly because yours is not the easiest hair to deal with but also because you are usually too busy to fiddle around with it. You may be sharp featured, especially when young, even slightly monkey-like but with a steady forward gaze which is full of Gemini curiosity. Your hands and feet are neat, and you try to maintain a rather stylish and youthful appearance throughout life. Your chic, attractive clothes reflect your busy super-modern lifestyle. Your car is an important part of your turnout, and this too would be small, neat, sporty and fast. Joan Collins is a good example of someone who looks typically Geminian. Her large eyes, small face, difficult hair and perennially youthful appearance are strong Gemini characteristics.

Outer manner
Your outer manner is cheerful, confident and friendly, but possibly sharp and off-putting to newcomers. Personally, I am rather nervous of Gemini rising subjects, your sarcastic and unfeeling outer manner can put me on the defensive. This is stupid of me because I know that the sharp-edged cleverness is a sham, a shield which protects your vulnerability and shaky sense of self-esteem. You can appear strong, efficient and businesslike but, if you feel threatened in any way, you can be cutting and hurtful. Females with this sign on the ascendant give an

appearance of capability and efficiency which doesn't seem to detract from their femininity. The Gemini rising mind is masculine and the mental processes are logical and orderly, more suited to the engineer or computer programmer than anyone's idea of a dizzy woman.

You use your hands while talking and may be emphatic when excited about something. You remain young looking throughout life. You may actually fear old age yourself, but your attitude and appearance guarantee that you remain youthful even in your old age. Your quick mind and sense of humour are delightful.

Gemini characteristics

This section can double up as a brief guide to Gemini as a sun sign *or* as a rising sign, so it provides a handy reference for you if you wish to check out someone's Sun sign as well as their rising sign.

Your movements are quick, you walk and talk quickly and appear to have little patience with those who can't keep up with you but this is misleading. Just because you think and act quickly doesn't necessarily mean that you lack patience with those who don't; on the contrary, you *expect* others to be slower than you and you take time to explain things to them in an orderly manner. You may well lack patience with people who avoid making any kind of effort or who are mentally lazy. However, your sense of humour and genuine interest in other people protects you from true hardness. Some weak people may be frightened off by your dynamism, while others are drawn towards it. At least you do take the trouble to *talk* to others.

Gemini rising subjects can be seen passing the time of day with children, the elderly and even the local pussy-cat; you even talk back to the television! You like to listen as well as to talk because you find people interesting. This ensures that you have many acquaintances. You are capable of a good deal of lateral thinking and you will listen to and take advice from those whom you respect.

Practically everything interests you; your curiosity leads you to ask about everything which is going on around you. You never stop learning and therefore pick up snippets of information on many subjects. This leads to the common accusation by astrologers that Geminians know a little about many subjects; the implication being that they know nothing in depth. I don't go along with this old saw. It's true that most Geminians have dustbin-like minds, but you are able to study in depth and may well know at least one subject thoroughly, even if is only the performance of your local football team.

You need mental stimulation and also seek to stimulate the minds of others. In social situations, you are considered to be witty, funny, friendly, clever and amusing. Usually very talkative, you may appear boastful at times, but your slight tendency to exaggerate is actually just a device which is used to entertain and amuse others or to push home a particular point. You hide behind humour, because this covers you when panic sets in or when you feel yourself to be out of your depth. Although this sign is not especially associated with actors, you can act a part to suit your circumstances, and you tend to keep your true feelings hidden. Think back to that difficult childhood where you were taught that your demands were unlikely to be met, and that your feelings were unlikely to be important to others.

You learned early how to get on with life and how to put up with emotional discomfort or to adapt yourself to the prevailing situation. However, despite your ability to adapt to difficult situations, you can't half moan about them! You must beware that you don't adopt the typically Geminian moany, whiny little voice.

There is a myth among non-astrologers that Geminians have split personalities, this remark often being accompanied by the comment that Gemini is the sign of the twins. But how about the two fish of Pisces or the two cups in Libra's weighing scales? I personally doubt that schizophrenia is especially reserved for Geminians. It is true that as a Gemini subject, you can do many different things, sometimes all at the same time, and you can often accomplish more in one day than anyone else can in a week. You can also vary your behaviour according to the company in which you find yourself, but you are not alone in that.

On the whole, Geminians are consistent even in their inconsistency and you are no less reliable than many other signs. Geminians are dextrous, you are clever when it comes to making, fixing and mending things but some Geminis go out of their way to avoid this kind of work due to the fact that they have been criticized or made to feel clumsy during childhood. I have a couple of female Gemini acquaintances who considered themselves useless when it came to practical matters because they had husbands who always 'knew better'. Eventually, a day came when they *had* to cope and, of course, they managed very well. Obviously, none of us know what we can do until we are up against it, but Geminis, when given the two-pennyworth of encouragement, are pretty capable people.

Some of you lack intellectual confidence and may consider studying to be beyond you. However, when you put your mind to a subject, you soon find that your brains are the equal of anyone else's. If you have Gemini very strongly on your chart, you could be a first-class fidget, never stopping still for long enough to accomplish anything and always moving on to something (or someone) new. If the Gemini traits are diluted by a few planets in earth and/or fixed signs, you will be able to think more deeply and achieve a balance between frenetic activity and concentrated effort. This type of Gemini subject translates his need to rise above the shortcomings of his childhood into achievement. It's worth bearing in mind that this is one of the most ambitious of all the Zodiac signs. Your worst enemies are your nerves and your fear of boredom and entrapment. A Gemini rising friend of mine pointed out that she can only cope with a job which offers variety and that doing the same thing all the time would drive her crazy.

The mid-heaven

This section and those which follow apply only to Gemini rising subjects. The mid-heaven can show the subject's aims and ambitions, his attitude to work and his public standing. Those who have an early degree of Gemini on the ascendant will have Capricorn on the mid-heaven, but all the rest (e.g. the majority of you) have Aquarius on the mid-heaven. Those of you who have Capricorn on the MC are ambitious and determined, looking for security and advancement. The majority of self-made multi-millionaires have Gemini strong in their charts, which proves the point that you often work harder than most people. You can put your mind to the job and get on with it in a way that other people can only envy. You can turn your selling and communicating skills to good account by sticking at a job and climbing slowly up the career ladder.

The earth sign quality of Capricorn suggests that you are probably attracted to work where the values are material, in business, banking and large corporations, because you feel a need to achieve something solid by your efforts. This combination could make you a highly skilled and ambitious operator. Alternatively, you could find a comfortable job and stick with it for years as long as there were plenty of new faces around for company and entertainment.

The vast majority of Gemini rising subjects, however, have Aquarius on the mid-heaven and this brings both vision and humanitarianism into the picture. There may be a measure of idealism in your choice of career and this, coupled with your need to communicate, leads you towards the whole area of teaching. Not all Gemini rising subjects train as teachers, of course, but my bet is that your job is bound to lead you into aspects of teaching or training somewhere along the way. If you follow any of the other typically Gemini careers such as sales representative, journalist, writer, broadcaster or telephonist, you will still try to help people, both on a personal day-to-day basis or by means of communicating useful or instructive ideas.

Gemini's ruling planet is Mercury. In mythology, the Roman god, Mercury, was a messenger who worked for all the gods, but especially for Apollo. Indeed he was Apollo's errand-boy and, as such, did a good deal of his boss's dirty work, often getting the blame or being 'dropped in it' by his ungrateful superior; a situation which is familiar even today! Another, more satisfying side of this god's work was healing, and this still draws Mercurial people even now. Strictly speaking, the healing attributes are often laid at the feet of the other Mercury-ruled sign of Virgo, but Geminians do their bit in their own way. The idealistic Aquarian mid-heaven coupled with the Geminian need to help can lead to a medical or nursing career, but the need to communicate often manifests itself in some kind of counselling work. Therefore, psychiatry, marriage guidance or the counselling side of astrology could appeal to you either as a full-time occupation or as a satisfying sideline.

The presence of such forward looking air signs on both the ascendant and mid-heaven gives an interest in computers, electronics, word-processing and also radar, radio, telephone communications and television, both from an engineering point of view and by working directly in the broadcasting field. The need to communicate over vast distances can even lead to an interest in the para-normal, mediumship and even more obviously, when one considers the *healing* emphasis, a talent for spiritual or 'faith' healing. Remember that Aquarius is a *fixed* sign, therefore your interests may be varied but you will stick with them throughout your life. Aquarius and Capricorn also bring a deep-seated need for status and public recognition.

The MC can throw some light on the kind of partners you choose both in business and in personal life. You may be attracted to people who reflect the values of the signs on your mid-heaven or who are actually born under those signs (e.g. Capricorns or Aquarians).

The descendant

The opposite point to the ascendant is the descendant or the cusp of the seventh house. Traditionally this is supposed to show the kind of person to whom we are attracted. When Gemini is rising, the descendant is in Sagittarius so, in theory, you should find yourself especially attracted to Sagittarians. In practice, you could be attracted to any one of the 12 signs – or none of them! Perhaps you look for Sagittarian values in your friends, or your approach to a prospective mate is Sagittarian in character. The Sagittarian values are intelligence, broad-mindedness and a taste for adventure.

This descendant denotes a need for personal freedom in relationships. You may or may not wish to try out different partners, but you do need to be free to come in and go out without being subjected to the third degree. You need to be able to follow a career or a particular leisure interest without your partner complaining of neglect. The Gemini need for *mental* stimulation plus space, suggests that the most successful partnership would be with someone who is equally involved with a career and who also has a measure of self-reliance.

When your nerves let you down, when your confidence evaporates, when the world suddenly makes you feel like the inept, incompetent, unwanted child you once were perceived to be, then you need a partner who will be there to reassure and comfort you, perhaps in a slightly motherly way. With Sagittarius on the descendant, you might not get all the love and reassurance that you need from a partner.

If your ascendant is late in Gemini, much of your seventh house will be in Capricorn which will encourage you to seek out a reliable and responsible kind of partner, perhaps one who is on his way to a position of power and influence.

Love, sex and relating – regardless of the descendant

This is above all a sign of the intellect, therefore a stimulating partner is a necessity. You can even put up with an absolute rat more easily than you can a boring partner. It hardly needs to be stressed that the old familiar triangle of 'safe partner and thrilling but unreliable lover', could have been made for you. Even a thrilling but unreliable partner is all right, just as long as you can still enjoy your first real loves which are your work and your hobbies!

Geminians are curious, so you probably experimented with sex quite early in life. I know one Gemini rising lady who, on being told that such-and-such a young man was 'dangerous', simply had to go and find out if it was true. There is an element of the 'don't die wondering' syndrome here, the source of which is the same kind of fiddle-fingered curiosity which leads you to pick spots.

To be honest, you *can* live without sex, as long as you are creatively occupied. Under extreme circumstances, you could go without it for at least four days, however your need for comfort and company will soon draw you back to companionship. Most of you are tuned into the needs of others which, alongside your famous dexterity and penchant for doing two things at once, makes you an inventive and exciting bed partner. Your greatest need is to communicate, therefore you are unlikely to be so tuned into your own needs that you don't also take into account the needs of a partner.

Health

Gemini rules the arms, shoulders, wrists and hands, also the bronchial tubes and lungs. Therefore, asthma, bronchitis and rheumatism are all possible complaints. Strained ligaments and broken wrists are common too. Your nerves are delicate so you could expect skin eruptions, allergies, migraine and nervous bowel problems. You may have an occasional spell of hysteria due to overstretched nerves, or as a result of too much worry. If ever a sign benefited from meditation, massage and relaxation techniques, this is the one.

Your sixth house is in Scorpio, so please also look at the health section on page 134.

CHAPTER 7

Cancer Rising

Keep the home fires burning, while
your hearts are yearning,
Though your lads are far away they
dream of home;
There's a silver lining through the dark
clouds shining,
Turn the dark cloud inside out, till the
boys come home.

Lena Guilbert Ford, *Keep the Home Fires
Burning*

A few words of explanation
A sign on the ascendant expresses itself in a different way from
a Sun sign. However, some of the characteristics, even the

childhood experiences, will apply if you have the Sun in Cancer or in the fourth house. They may be present if you have the Moon in Cancer or the fourth house because the Moon is a strong influence on any chart and it is the natural ruler of the sign of Cancer. If the ascendant is weak (see Chapter 1), the Cancer overlay will not be so noticeable. If the rest of the birthchart is very different from the rising sign, there could be a conflict within the personality. This is because the outer manner, the signals which are given out at first meeting by the subject are very different from the main underlying character. Another possibility is that the subject rejects all that his parents and parent figures stood for and creates a life which is very different from the one which they envisaged for him or the one which he lived through as a child.

Cancer is a feminine/negative sign which belongs to the water group but we must remember that it is a cardinal sign which implies a certain underlying decisiveness. Even though Cancer is deemed to be a gentle sign, oriented towards the feminine principles of home and family, people with this sign rising know what they want and will not be made to do without it for long. This is a sign of long ascension, therefore there are many people with this sign on the ascendant, at least in the northern hemisphere.

Early experiences
As I said in the previous paragraph, there are many people born with this sign rising which is nice because, thankfully, it represents a fairly pleasant childhood. The chances are that you were well cared for by at least one of your parents and never left for long periods with other people or badly treated. Very few people have a perfect childhood and one could argue that a completely trouble-free childhood is a poor training for adult life. It is better if a little rain *does* fall from time to time, so that one learns to use an umbrella later on! Your childhood had a few showers, so to speak, but it was far from being a deluge of misery. This sign is especially associated with the mother, mother-figure or anybody who took on the nurturing role.

Your childhood home would have been fairly comfortable

with a slight emphasis on materialism, but not as much as in the case of Taurus or Libra rising where the emphasis was on *things* rather than feelings. You were a wanted child, possibly the first one born into the family and you were able to have your parent's exclusive attention for a few years at least. Maybe you were the youngest child, being allowed to stay young while the others were encouraged to grow up more quickly.

You had a responsible attitude to life and a slightly dignified manner. You didn't get into any ridiculous escapades and neither did you find it necessary to play the part of the clown. You were quiet and rather cautious, a bit inclined to cling to home and mother and reluctant to move on out into the world. This attitude tends to change later in life as the ascendant progresses from cautious Cancer into adventurous Leo.

There is some evidence of religious or spiritual messages being handed out by your parents and these are accepted or rejected later in life according to your changing views and circumstances. I personally tend to see this very much as a Jewish rising sign; just think of the traditional relationship between the Jewish mother and her children! A quick survey of my Jewish friends confirms that there is a particularly high incidence of this ascendant. In non-Jewish families, the Cancerian ascendant does seem to lead to a faint whiff of religious or moral pressure being put on the child; in short, the child is urged to conform with the parent's ideological outlook. This doesn't pose much of a problem because the Cancerian is conformist by nature.

In all probability, you had a good relationship with your father but he might have been a slightly remote figure, being wrapped up in his work or personal interests. Some Cancer rising subjects have a sneaking contempt for their fathers, considering them to be weak willed or wimpish. In some cases, the father becomes seriously ill either in a dramatic way which frightens the child, or in a lingering way which requires some kind of permanent care and attention. One Cancer rising friend of mine told me that his father had a weak and frequently ulcerated stomach which meant the father needed to eat very carefully whilst also being protected from worry. This ensured that the

mother was the power in the family, so reinforcing the typical
Cancerian respect for the power of the mother. Incidentally,
unless there are hard aspects from the planet Saturn to your
ascendant, you were probably born very easily.

Many Cancer rising subjects experience some kind of
problem in connection with their schooling, especially during
the secondary or college phase of their education. This stems
more from peer group pressure than actual education problems.
You were probably rather slow and lazy when young, being more
inclined to sit and dream rather than to get down to work.
However, your desire to conform and a growing awareness that
the road to adult success begins with school achievement,
ensures that you catch up later and leave your earlier classmates
behind. This increase of academic speed may bring a jealous
and spiteful response from your erstwhile and soon-to-be-left-
behind friends. You don't seem to go through the same kind of
rebellious phase as other teenagers, thereby further alienating
yourself from your peers, for a while at least.

There is some evidence that the famed Cancerian attitude of
obedience to parental wishes doesn't last forever. The evidence
is that you will eventually quietly but firmly reject your parent's
preferences in favour of a career or lifestyle of your own choice.
A Cancer rising client of mine gave up an intended career in
medicine by dropping out half-way through the course and
taking a job in a shop. When asked why he had done this, he
replied that he realized that medicine was his *parents'* choice and
that he really needed to find out for himself how he really
wanted to live and what he was really fitted for. Despite these
changes of direction, you tend to remain affectionately close to
your parents throughout their lives.

Appearance
Cancer rising subjects are attractive rather than beautiful, with
chubby features, full cheeks and lips and a nicely shaped nose.
Your chest and rib cage are large and your shoulders and arms
well covered. This gives males a slightly top heavy look, while
females frequently have an hourglass type of figure. In white
races, the skin is pale and the hair can range from mid-brown to

almost black, and it is usually strong and abundant, with a will of its own. Your height is probably small to average, and you have to watch your weight later in life. Your hands and feet are small and neat. Both sexes with this ascendant like to look after their appearance and women hate to go out without make-up and nail polish. Both sexes prefer to wear conservative clothes in plain colours. Garish patterns and checks are not liked at all.

Outer manner
Women with this ascendant appear very feminine and rather cuddly. Men appear kind, gentle and equally cuddly. Both sexes are popular because they are pleasant, kindly and humorous. The strange thing is that you do not really seek friendship and are not terribly interested in people outside your immediate family. Most Cancer rising subjects get over their early shyness and become outgoing adults, often with a talent for sales-manship and the more pleasant kind of company politics. You prefer to pour oil on troubled waters than to stir up a storm. You are a bit shy, being rather modest and retiring in new company. You hate to look outrageous, to draw attention to yourself or to make a public fool of yourself. You obey the rules, and are generally very civilized in your manner. You are good to talk to because you are such a good listener but your habit of questioning others may be a bit too intrusive to some people.

Cancer characteristics
In the case of Cancer rising, the Moon assumes a greater level of importance than is usual because it is associated with the sign of Cancer and is, therefore, the chart ruler. It will be especially strong if in the sign of Cancer and/or in the first house or in the fourth house.

My questionnaire revealed that Cancerians consider that they remain *themselves* in all situations. They tell me that they don't vary their behaviour to suit the company in which they find themselves. As an outside observer, I don't entirely agree with this. You are definitely not two-faced, you don't tell one thing to one person and something else to another, neither do you go to pains to put on an act, but you do behave differently in different settings. When out at work or with friends, you are friendly, chatty, charming and apparently confident. If someone takes it upon themselves to patronize or criticize you, this results in you immediately clamming up – it is worth remembering that your memory is very good and that you rarely forgive or forget a hurt. In the home you can vary between being cheerful, loving and considerate, sulky and withdrawn, or cross and irritable.

Like your Taurean cousins, you are pretty foul to be around if you are cold and hungry and only a complete fool would try to tackle you on some contentious subject the moment you walked in the door after a hard day's work. Later on when you have had time to eat, relax and digest your meal, you can be safely approached! Your worst fault is your tendency to switch off and retreat into yourself. For instance, if something goes wrong at work, you can come home in a bad mood and stay that way for several weeks! By the time your spouse begins to suggest divorce proceedings, you have completely forgotten what put you in the mood in the first place. Another fault is your parsimony. No one is more careful with money, except for a Piscean.

You prefer to make up your own mind about everything and cannot be dictated to. This, of course, is what one would expect of a cardinal sign. You can be slow to make up your mind about people and you don't trust snap judgements, not even your own. Unless you are under intense pressure, you can be comfortable anywhere; however, you prefer classy people and clean, comfortable surroundings. Your senses are strong, especially the senses of hearing and smell, you cannot stand noisy and smelly surroundings.

You are sensible and realistic, preferring to solve problems in a practical manner than to analyse and agonize over them for any length of time. In fact, you shy away from any intense examination of feelings; you have no patience with people who insist on studying their own navels for hours on end. You fear emotional stress and become ill if you have to face too much of it. You may even appear unsympathetic to the troubles of others, but the truth is that your psychic skin is very thin, and you automatically shy away from too much drama in an effort to protect yourself.

You love having people around you, both the family and your

work colleagues, but you do need to recharge your psychic batteries by spending a bit of time alone on occasion. Going for a walk, doing a few chores in the garden or having a late lay-in are all ways in which you do this. You dislike housework but can make use of it to give you space and peace from the demands of others. Another peculiarity is that you can take any amount of noise and panic at work but you do need a peaceful and tension-free atmosphere at home. If forced into an argument in any sphere of your life, you can be surprisingly blunt and hurtful. You observe more than other people realize, but you tend to keep your observations to yourself, so it is only when challenged that you show just how well you know your opponent.

Most astrology books stress the traditional Cancerian closeness to the home and the family, and this is true. You don't like living alone. You enjoy an afternoon of your own company but you really can't manage for long without some kind of companionship. You are naturally domesticated and probably quite a skilled cook. Although very attentive to the needs of your family, you also need life outside the home. You prefer a job which is both steady and secure but which also gives you a measure of authority and autonomy. Remember this is a cardinal sign which suggests that you are a good decision maker. You like to do your job properly and can be relied upon to complete a project unsupervised. You have a natural affinity to the world of business and enjoy managing or running a business of your own.

Your outlook and values tend to be traditional. The chances are that your parents were sensible and you probably find it quite easy to follow their example. You need a secure base; a home of your own with your family around – you hate to part company with any relative, however demanding or cantankerous they may become. You will drop friends and acquaintances however, if they begin to take the mickey out of you or to make jokes at your expense. Your sense of humour and tolerance of human nature disappears the minute a 'wind-up merchant' comes along to prick your dignity.

Your tastes are simple; you enjoy good food and drink, good

company, books, music and the scent of flowers. Many of you are voracious readers, often sticking to one or two preferred kinds of book. History is liked and you may be quite a knowledgeable amateur historian. The collecting instinct is not so noticeable in the rising sign as it is with Sun in Cancer but you join your Cancer Sun sign cousins in hating to throw anything away. Your senses are strong – discordant sounds offend you but not nearly as much as bad smells. Oddly enough, you don't follow the current fad for complaining about the smell of other people's cigarettes. You love to travel, especially by water, but your weak stomach makes you a poor sailor. You need access to a car; if possible you want to buy your own car because you feel frustrated if you cannot get up and go whenever you feel inclined.

The mid-heaven

People who were born in the UK, northern Europe and Canada may have one of three mid-heavens, while people born in southern Europe and the USA have a choice of two. The correct placement of the MC, like everything else in astrology, demands an accurate date, time and place of birth. The most usual MC in Britain and most northerly latitudes is Pisces, whereas in the USA and southern Europe Pisces and Aries are equally possible. A very few northern births may result in an Aquarius MC.

Cancer/Aquarius

There is some conflict here because Cancer seeks security while Aquarius seeks freedom. In resolving this conflict, you may behave in one way dealing with friends and family and in another pursuing your worldly ambitions. If the signs are allowed to blend rather than conflict with one another, you could be drawn to one of the caring professions due to the fact that these are both caring signs. Counselling work is a possibility, as is medicine, veterinary work and, of course, teaching. Another talent which these signs share is the ability to buy and sell. Cancer wants to drive a hard bargain, while Aquarius wants to be friends with the world but both signs are adept at looking friendly while hiding their true thoughts and feelings. The intuitive skills of astrology, palmistry, graphology, numerology and the Tarot etc. may appeal to you, possibly enough to make a part-time or full-time living from them. Political activity is a natural for you, so you could be drawn to work in the civil service, local government or you may choose to serve on committees.

Cancer/Pisces

This mixture produces a sentimental person for whom continuity is important. You probably prefer to stay in a job where you feel yourself to be appreciated as part of a successful team. The Pisces element can bring confusion regarding your aims, so you could drift along, hoping for the best rather than reaching for a specific goal. If Neptune (the ruler of Pisces), is well aspected in the chart, career muddles will be less of a problem. The travel trade may attract you, or you may have to travel in connection with some other type of work. The combination does not usually bring any burning ambitions; you just want a happy working life and contentment at home. Some of you may not actually go out to work, preferring to work from home or spend your energies looking after children or animals.

This combination brings an interest in healing, so you may work in the medical or the alternative medical fields. Just to digress for a moment, all the Cancer/Pisces people whom I know seem to consult alternative medical practitioners either in addition to, or in place of conventional doctors. Whether personally involved or not, you find it quite easy to accept the idea of spiritual healing and psychic or mediumistic work, probably due to your own natural highly developed level of intuition. You have a natural affinity with money and budgeting, therefore finance work (which also requires intuition) and fund raising for a charity are possible interests.

Cancer/Aries

This combination brings together two cardinal signs, so you would be unlikely to blindly follow any course of action which was against your own interests. The charm of the Cancerian ascendant masks your wilfulness to some extent. You could make a good politician or diplomat because you appear to be sociable and reasonable, but you are usually able to make your point. If you want to, you can push your way to the top by sheer hard work and by keeping your goals clearly in sight, however some of you are too lazy to make the effort.

You probably prefer self-employment to being part of a team and may be interested in a mixture of the rather muscular Aries type of job and the gentler, more domestic, Cancerian type. This could lead you to run a small building concern, or to employ a group of gardening contractors or a battalion of office cleaners. Both Cancer, which is associated with patriotism and history, plus Aries which has military inclinations, lead to an interest in military matters. This could suggest a career in the services (especially the navy) or part-time involvement with a para-military organization. You might be interested in the Scout movement or something similar. Whatever you choose to do, you won't allow the grass to grow under your feet.

General comments

Cancerians are often good cooks, so you might work in the fields of catering or of dietetics. Your need to help others can lead to teaching or nursing, although you may not have the stomach for some kinds of medical work.

Many subjects are drawn to those who have their Sun in the subject's mid-heaven sign, so you could be attracted to Aquarian, Piscean or Arian types according to the position of your MC.

The descendant

The opposite point to the ascendant is the descendant, or the cusp of the seventh house. Traditionally this is supposed to show the type of person to whom we are attracted. When Cancer is rising, the descendant is Capricorn so in theory, you should find yourself attracted to Capricorn people. In practice, you could be attracted to any one of the 12 signs but you may look for friends and associates who have Capricornian attributes or you may approach others in a Capricornian manner.

This descendant denotes a need for safe and secure relationships. You are sincere in your dealings with others and you seek the same sincerity from others. You need a practical partner who can stand on his own feet and who has a sense of personal dignity. You are very caring and dutiful in your attitude to others, even when the relationship is a detached one such as a close colleague at work. You don't appreciate people whose eccentricities include a lack of personal principles, laziness or stupidity; you appreciate efficiency. You may be attracted to a partner who is ambitious or outstanding. Then having found your high-flyer, set out to curb or control them in some way.

I have not noticed any prevalence of Cancer/Capricorn marriages; however, these two signs have much in common so this could work quite well. Both signs are family minded, therefore both would understand the other's attachment to his own family. Parents, in-laws and grandparents will be looked after by both parties whenever necessary. The cautious attitude suggested by this descendant makes you slow to begin experimenting with relationships and inclined to marry later in life than usual. When you do commit yourself, however, you do so wholeheartedly.

Love, sex and relating – regardless of the descendant

Your caution and shyness means that you are slow to get off the ground in this area of life; many of you seem to wait until your thirties before marrying and having children, but when you do, your intentions are that you stay married, preferably for life. It is possible that this very sense of commitment is one reason for your hesitancy. Another peculiarity of this rising sign is that you are probably most comfortable with a partner who is quite a bit younger or older than yourself. You are protective towards your partner but you may take this a bit too far, becoming a bit of a mother hen.

This is not a notably sexy sign. Comments which came in on the questionnaires such as 'an affectionate cuddle is as important to me as sex' and 'I see sex as being part of a larger relationship rather than as an end in itself' are typical. You need to love and be loved and to have the love of a family around you, and this includes parents, siblings and children. You are potty about your own children and can also give a great deal of love and affection to other people's children. Some Cancer rising women unfortunately seem to lose their fragile sexuality as soon as the babies come along, it seems that once the goal of motherhood has been reached, they have no more real use for their sex drive. If the Cancerian lady is shrewd (and I haven't met one yet who wasn't) she will try to re-activate this side of herself in order to keep the interest of her husband and to prevent him straying. Sex at its best for you is a mixture of love, physical contact, affectionate play and a pleasurable release of energy; it is rarely an end in itself. Your strong senses lead you to enjoy music, flowers and a good meal with much the same relish as you enjoy sex. When in a loving relationship which is fairly free of money worries, you are contentedly sexy; otherwise you can do without it – for a while at least. An urge which is far more powerful than sex for you is to find a partner who shares your values, interests, and beliefs.

Health
Traditionally the areas which give you trouble are the stomach, breasts and the lower end of the lungs. Many Cancer rising subjects seem to have weak throats and also suffer from rheumatism. I can work out the reason for the rheumatism because it is a reflection from the Capricorn descendant, but I cannot see any astrological reason for your weak throats, even though they nevertheless seem to be there.

Your sixth house is in Sagittarius, so please also look at the health section on page 147.

CHAPTER 8
Leo Rising

I suppose that means that I shall have to die beyond my means.

Oscar Wilde
—on being presented with a Doctor's fee for an operation

A few words of explanation

A sign on the ascendant expresses itself in a different way from a Sun sign; however, some of the characteristics, even the childhood experiences, might apply if you have the Sun in Leo or in the fifth house. They may be present if you have the Sun in the first house and even, to some extent, if you have the Moon in Leo, although the Moon rules the emotions and the reactions rather than one's conscious day-to-day activities. If the ascendant is weak (see Chapter 1), the Leo overlay will not be so noticeable. If the rest of the birthchart is different in character, there could be a conflict within the personality. This is because the outer manner, the signals which are given out by the subject on first meetings, are very different from the underlying personality. Another possibility is that the subject rejects all that his parents, teachers and parent figures stood for and creates a life which is very different from theirs.

Leo is a masculine, positive sign which is fixed in quality, therefore the subject will present a confident, capable and reliable image to the world. This is a sign of long ascension which implies that there are a lot of these people about but, oddly enough, we seem to run across far fewer Leo rising subjects in daily life than we do their immediate neighbours of Cancer and Virgo rising. There is no astrological reason for this discrepancy but there may be a few less obvious ones.

Firstly, Leo rising infants are not strong and don't all survive the first months of infancy. Secondly, these subjects don't seem to lead ordinary lives; they become captains of industry, sports champions or stars in the entertainment world, which suggests that they are not to be found in the local pub or at the office. Thirdly, this is a royal sign and is actually well represented as either a Sun sign, rising sign or Moon sign within the royal family. The few members of the 'nobility and gentry' whom I have come across invariably have Leo strongly placed on their charts, so once again these types are not likely to abound at one's local garage or under the dryer in the hairdressers. All in all, this sign carries a pedigree!

Early experiences

The chances are that your parents wanted you and valued your presence in their life from the day you were born, but this doesn't suggest that everything in your childhood was rosy. Your father (or anyone taking on the paternal role) would have had an old-fashioned, rather authoritarian attitude. You were encouraged to develop your talents and abilities but also to conform to rather set patterns of thought and behaviour. Your parents were traditional in outlook, probably following some kind of religious belief in a ritualistic and traditional manner. This is not because they 'saw the light' or were 'born again', but because they themselves followed their own family traditions. If you were born with this ascendant, you could have come from a family of practising Roman Catholics, Anglo-catholics, Jews, Moslems or any other respectable, traditional and rather authoritarian religion. The chances are that later in life, you questioned your parents' beliefs, finally finding some kind of philosophy or religious outlook which was better suited to your own views. You would be unlikely to live without some kind of personal belief.

Your parental home was probably comfortable and your parents fairly well off. They may not have been rich but they would have been respectable. It is most unlikely that you came from a broken home, because your parents believed in staying together and working out their problems within the family. Although home life was comfortable and, on the whole, peaceful, you do not seem to have been spoiled or over-indulged as a child because you were expected to behave in a reasonable and responsible manner.

There is usually something weird about the childhood when Leo is rising and this same quality of weirdness may also be experienced by the Sun in Leo children. As a child you would have been imbued with messages which told you that you were in some way special – you doubtless also experienced feelings of isolation. Your parents may have favoured you because you were the first child to be born to the family, the only child, or a child of one sex in a family mainly composed of the opposite one. You may have been a much-loved late addition, born when your parents had time and money to spare; therefore right from the beginning, you learned to stand slightly apart.

Leonine children are often talented; some are academic, some artistic, others are creative, sporty or even mediumistic. A talented child, especially if he comes from a non-talented family, always stands a little apart from the others and this is even more likely if his talent is consciously fostered by the parents. This slight sense of isolation is less noticeable when the rest of the birthchart inclines the child towards good relationships. Leos are warm and friendly creatures who love to give and receive affection and this suggests that you manage to overcome any slight difficulties which this sense of specialness might have given you.

Your relationship with your mother was probably very good but your father may have been an authoritarian figure. He could have been distant and even rather frightening. If you were lucky, you compensated for this by becoming close to a grandparent or a favourite uncle. It may have been difficult for you to make friends at school, especially if you were accustomed to spending your spare time with adults. There is, as with all fixed signs on the ascendant, a slightly watchful air about you, but this is nothing compared to the barriers which are associated with some of the other rising signs.

Appearance
Remember to make allowances for racial differences when looking at astrological appearances. Leo risers are quite distinctive, usually tall and well built, with a slow and regal way of moving. Both sexes are vain and will go to a lot of trouble to look good. You worry about your hair which is probably thick and abundant. Both sexes prefer to wear their hair long. Leo men are terrified they might lose their hair and may spend hours worrying about this. You like to dress fashionably, even glamorously, and to surround yourself with quality goods. A good car is an essential addition to your turnout.

Outer manner
Leos have a regal deportment, the head is often held high and the pace of movements are slow, even measured. You are genuinely interested in people and present a kindly, non-hostile personality to the world. You can appear arrogant and demanding, even unrealistic at times, but for the most part you are liked and admired. Leos have presence, graciousness and inborn public relations skills. You are a good listener and an interesting talker which makes you popular in social situations. You are quite fussy about your choice of friends, and this is where a touch of the Leo snobbery can often be seen.

Leo characteristics
This section can double up as a brief guide to Leo as a Sun sign

or as a rising sign, so it can provide a handy reference if you want to check up on someone's Sun sign as well as their rising sign.

Leos prefer to live and work at a steady pace, often getting a lot done without rushing; indeed, you hate being rushed and hustled as this makes you irritable, even angry. Some of you are content to peg along doing your own thing, but many of you rise naturally to positions of responsibility and authority which you carry off very well. When in charge of others you rarely cause them to be resentful, but you can be bossy, arrogant and overbearing when under stress. Your attitude in the home is much the same, being loving, responsible and kind but needing to be respected by those around you. As a parent, you are sensible and responsible. You may spoil your children a little but you will not stand for rudeness or uncivilized behaviour.

You enjoy living in a grand manner and are quite prepared to work hard for the money you need. Money for its own sake doesn't interest you, but home comforts, a good holiday, a nice car and the wherewithal to provide yourself and your family with entertainment certainly does. Your home is bound to be attractive, possibly even impressive; it may not be terribly tidy but it is comfortable and structurally sound. You like space, large rooms and a bit of land around you, indeed you prefer to live in the country rather than in town. You do need to be on a good commuter route because you enjoy nipping into the city from time to time. My Leo rising friend, Malcolm, is a good example of this. He has always lived in the West Country but in his youth commuted up to London to play in a jazz band. Nowadays he travels up to town to work at the occasional psychic exhibition or on various other kinds of business.

Most Leos are fond of animals, especially cats. You are also fond of company, therefore your home is never silent or lonely. You need to be excited about life by becoming involved with either your job, hobby or sporting interests. You enjoy competition and also a good-natured dispute with your many friends. If you are a typical Leo, you will have a tendency to hold court and to treat a group of people as an audience. However, you are so entertaining that they rarely resent this.

You probably married while you were quite young. Leos on

the whole have a good track record where marriage is concerned, preferring to stay with a partner and make things work rather than to flit irresponsibly from one partner to another. However, when this sign is on the ascendant, the descendant (the opposite point to the ascendant) is in the volatile sign of Aquarius, which throws a different complexion on things, but more of this later in the ascendant/descendant section. If you are forced to leave a partner, you don't go off the idea of relationships altogether but hope one day to meet someone else with whom you can live in trust and comfort. This preference for stability also extends to your working life and your friendships. You stick to people and situations and, in practical terms, you prefer to finish anything which you start. Your values could, by today's standards, be considered old-fashioned.

Leonine people love to travel, preferably in five-star comfort. Travel in connection with work is made for you because you were born to have an expense account. You are an excellent organizer, a kind of walking Filofax. You can organize your own day and also the work of others and fortunately, you make a popular if fairly demanding boss. Your enthusiasm, faith in the future and occasional headstrong leaps into impossible situations are an inspiration to others, even if a trifle wearing to your family. Your sense of humour, optimism and kindness makes you popular. You have an air of competence, even of invincibility; but your family, who see you a bit more clearly, know that you can have bouts of quite severe depression when something occurs which knocks your confidence. Nevertheless, even if you do become downhearted or angry, this won't last for long as you soon bounce back in order to get on with what you see as the game of life.

If challenged or made to feel inadequate in any way, you react by becoming pompous and putting on an air of self-importance. Try to avoid this if you can as it can have the effect of making you look even sillier. Although you have an excellent sense of humour, you are touchy. You don't appreciate having the mickey taken out of you and, if someone decides that you would make a good Aunt Sally, they soon find that they have taken on more than they have bargained for.

There are a couple of interesting observations which I would like to make before leaving this section, the first being that Leos can be mean! The sign is noted for is generosity and, true enough, some of you are the soul of generosity but many of you are quite the opposite! It is also wrong to say that Leos are over-dramatic. To be sure, you can put on a drama, especially if you are angry, but you can't compete with either Scorpio or Pisces when it comes to making a real scene. However, you are both proud and at the same time insecure, which means that you *hate* to be criticized.

The mid-heaven

This section and those which follow apply only to Leo rising subjects. The mid-heaven can show the subject's aims and ambitions, his attitude to work and his public standing. If Leo is rising, you could have either Aries or Taurus on the MC. The Leo/Aries combination adds sparkle to the chart as both are fire signs. The fixed/fire quality of Leo together with the cardinal/fire quality of Aries make for an ambitious, determined and capable person who attacks his goals with considerable enthusiasm. The Leo/Taurus combination shares the fact that both are fixed signs, therefore the person is less overtly ambitious but far more stubborn, determined and practical. Now let's take a deeper look at each combination on its own.

Leo/Aries

This combination inclines you towards self-employment, management positions and team leadership. In short, you're probably the boss. Being a faceless member of a team is not really your scene and therefore, even when joining an organization as a junior member, you stand out from the others and very soon begin to climb up the promotion ladder. You may not appear ambitious in the normal sense of the word, but you seem to drift towards the top, as if it were your rightful place in life. You enjoy success, status symbols and the feeling of being looked up to. The careers which may draw you are engineering, building and the driving of trains, planes and road vehicles. You could be an actor, teacher or jeweller – or a combination of these. You work at a steady pace but with periods of sheer idleness in between. Needless to say, most of the time you manage to achieve a great deal. It is possible that you will decide to 'drop out' at some later stage in your life, preferring a quiet lifestyle as a country gentleman. However, you can be relied upon to make sure that you can afford to do this beforehand.

Leo/Taurus

This makes for success just as long as you don't completely give in to your tendency for laziness. Both signs dislike change and prefer the continuity of a settled job. Both are quite ambitious even if this is not obvious. You can work at a job purely for the money it brings in or for the power and influence you might obtain from it; however you are happiest when your work contains a creative element. Both signs are creative and musical, so you could find work in the fields of fashion, art, music, engineering design, landscape gardening or catering. Your creativity could lead you to start a business of your own or, if you are not career minded, to create a lovely home of your own. If your job doesn't give you an opportunity for creativity, you will look for a creative hobby. You could grow prize plants and vegetables in your garden or you could add to your considerable popularity by being the neighbourhood's best cook.

Before leaving the career and aptitudes section of the MC, I would like to include a fact which my friend Denise has noticed. It occurred to her that people who have a strong dose of Leo on their birthchart get on very well with new technology such as word-processors, computers and computerized telex machines. Soon after Denise spotted this phenomenon, she did a head count around the offices where she works and sure enough, those people who really enjoyed using machinery all had either Sun, Moon or ascendant in Leo. After she told me this, I did my own head count and came up with the same answer. Neither of us can think of an astrological reason for this, except perhaps for the fact that Leos never really grow up and enjoy playing with toys all through their lives.

Some people are attracted to those whose Sun signs are the

same as their MC sign. This would suggest that the partner is in tune with the subject's aims and ambitions. In your case, you get on well both at work and in your personal life, with Aries or Taurus people.

The descendant

When the ascendant is in Leo, the opposite point or descendant is in Aquarius. There is no evidence to suggest that Leo rising subjects are particularly inclined to marry Aquarians but you may be attracted to Aquarian qualities in a partner. These qualities are independence, humanity and an individual outlook on life. You may treat your partner in a slightly Aquarian manner, thereby giving him space and freedom to be himself. You are incredibly difficult to please because you prefer a partner who is capable, independent and intrinsically fascinating, but at the same time you cannot stand too much competition. One Leo rising friend told me that he had given up a highly exciting relationship with a young woman because she was so clever and resourceful that she made him feel inadequate by comparison. You are choosy with regard to whom you call friends, but once somebody becomes a friend your loyalty towards them is almost completely unshakeable.

This Aquarian descendant can cause problems due to the unstable and revolutionary nature of the sign. In terms of relationships, this means that you are quite likely to be married more than once, possibly to partners who are rather odd. In some cases, your partners seem to start out normal and become odd at some later date!

Love, sex and relating – regardless of the descendant

You are truly a family person, but you cannot subordinate yourself too far to the wishes of a partner because you need to be treated with respect. If you feel that your role is important, either as wage-earner or home-maker and that your decisions count for something within the home, all is well. You need to love and be loved, and the love which you seek takes every form, including the love of your children, genuine care and affection for your mate and, of course, the satisfaction of your sexual desires. Hopefully this can be accomplished with your mate, but if it doesn't work out that way you are quite able to cope with a bit of extra-marital bliss.

Sexually, you are warm, caring, gentle and at the same time, demanding. You have a well-developed sense of touch and therefore will enjoy the relaxed sensuality of love-making rather than just looking for the pleasurable relief of an orgasm. You may not be all that ambitious when it comes to sexual acrobatics, but the act of love with a few interesting variations is, in your opinion, a better way of spending a couple of hours than most. Your technique is unhurried and your habitual attitude is generous and caring towards your partner. I cannot imagine anyone having any complaints and you are unlikely to complain if you are loved, cared for and made love to by someone whom you love and respect.

Any form of ridicule on the part of your partner would spell out the death of the relationship. You cannot bear to be ridiculed or embarrassed either in public or in private in respect of your body or your sexual performance. When things work out well, you are the most generous, kind, loyal and genuine partner that anyone can have.

Health
Leo is traditionally associated with the back and the heart. The husband of a friend of mine has his Sun in Leo and has had operations for spinal problems and a couple of heart attacks along the way. These ailments are not much fun, but they are typically Leonian in being traumatic and dramatic.

Your sixth house is in Capricorn, so please also look at the health section on page 160.

CHAPTER 9

Virgo Rising

Men of England wherefore plough
For the lords who lay ye low?
Wherefore weave with toil and care
The rich robes your tyrants wear?

Percy Bysshe Shelley, *Song to the
Men of England*

A few words of explanation

A sign on the ascendant expresses itself in a different way from a
Sun sign; however some of the characteristics and even the
childhood experiences will apply if you have the Sun in Virgo or
in the sixth house. They may also be present if you have
Mercury in Virgo or in the sixth house. If your Moon is in Virgo
or in the sixth house, your emotions and reactions will have a

Virgoan flavour. If the ascendant is weak (see Chapter 1), the Virgo overlay will not be so noticeable.

If the rest of the birthchart is very different from the rising sign there could be a conflict within the personality. This is because the outer manner, the signals which are given out at first meeting by the subject, is very different from the main character which lies underneath. Another possibility is that the subject rejects all that his parents and teachers stood for and creates a life for himself which is very different from the one which they envisaged for him or the one which he lived through as a child.

Remember that this sign is mutable which implies flexibility of mind and is an earth sign which suggests practicality, while also being feminine/negative in nature which implies introversion. Virgo rising is a sign of long ascension, which means that there are plenty of you around.

Early experiences
One of the questions on my research questionnaire asked 'would you like to have your childhood over again?' All but one of the Virgo rising respondents replied 'No, definitely not!' The only one who gave a 'yes' answer had her rising sign on the Virgo/Libra cusp. This is such a difficult ascendant to be born with that if your childhood was abnormally *happy* I'd suggest that you re-check your birth time!

Your parental home may have been comfortable or it may have been spartan, but whether your family was rich or poor, their attitude to the spending of money was probably frugal. This is assuming that you were brought up in a normal nuclear family. It is possible that you spent time being looked after by other people. And if your parents were particularly difficult, this could have been a blessing in disguise. It is quite common for a Virgo rising subject to have quite a good relationship with his mother but a difficult one with his father. In some cases, the father takes delight in tormenting or bullying the Virgo rising child. I'm not saying that all Virgo rising children go through this kind of experience but it is not that uncommon. In some cases, the father loves the child unreservedly but the mother cannot see any good in him (or more likely her) which leads to the child growing up under a constant barrage of criticism, knowing that whatever she does, she is never going to win her mother's approval. Not every case is as extreme as this, but the chances are that if you have this sign on the ascendant, you would have been on the receiving end of totally unfair and undeserved ill-treatment at the hands of others – most probably from just the people you should have been most able to trust.

Your parents were probably quite dutiful in their attitude towards you, making sure that you had your practical needs catered for. If they did this out of a sense of obligation rather than genuine affection, you would have been aware of this and you may even have felt guilty for putting them to the trouble of looking after you! You were expected to conform to a set of rules and regulations and to be clean and tidy at all times with polished shoes and straight, unwrinkled socks. Your school may also have been over-disciplined with too much emphasis on stuffy rules. I recall one Virgo rising lady telling me that she remembered being severely punished at school for turning up with the wrong coloured ribbons in her hair – and all this at the age of seven!

Your parents expected you to do well at school, to behave perfectly and to maintain a position at the top of the class at all times. This constant pressure and the unremitting requirement for you to be perfect at everything (except maybe for those subjects they themselves felt were unnecessary) could have left you rigid with nerves and shyness and prey to all kinds of nervous ailments. On the positive side, you had access to books, educational aids and extra-curricular activities. You were encouraged to read and to learn; and if you are typical of the sign, you probably got the hang of this quite early on. Your well-behaved manner endeared you to teachers and your modesty was inoffensive to the other children. You probably didn't try hard to make or keep friends, being happiest in your own company or with your pets; neither did you take much interest in any of the contemporary fads and fancies in which the other children were involved.

You have a surprisingly stubborn and uncompromisingly

selfish streak which may not be immediately obvious to others. Your survival instincts are strong, endowing you with a knack of appearing to be accommodating while actually pleasing yourself. You may have developed into an eccentric and uncompromising adult, preferring to live and work alone or among your pet animals. This may be the result of the unfair and unreasonable treatment you suffered as a child or it may be something which is purely a product of your personality. Some Virgo rising children actually resist love and affection, behaving so oddly and in such an offensive manner that nobody can really take to them.

Some Virgo rising subjects grow up in an overbearing religious atmosphere where the fear of God is added to the fear of what the neighbours might think. (This is especially so when the fourth house is in Sagittarius.) One Virgo rising friend of mine grew up in a Salvation Army family where everything was made subservient to religion.

Appearance
Virgo rising subjects are good looking as a rule, especially if they are born with a fairly late degree of the sign rising. You are probably a little taller than average with a long slim well-defined face and large pale eyes. All this has to be considered alongside racial differences and the influence of the rest of the chart. Typical subjects have a cheery smile and an intelligent sense of humour which shines out of the eyes. Your complexion is pale, even in the Summer, because you haven't the patience to waste time lolling around in the sun. You may be a little overweight or even thin with a bit of a pot-belly, but your above-average height and your good posture allows you to get away with this.

Outer manner
Your outer manner is polite, formal and a little guarded. You can hang back and be shy on first meeting, especially in new social circumstances but you soon warm up when you relax. Unless the rest of the chart is made up of pure 'pudding', your mind is very sharp and you can be surprisingly intuitive. You always *appear* confident and capable; the very image of the perfect purchasing officer, secretary or nurse. Being shy, you may also appear to be a little stand-offish on first acquaintance

and you prefer to let others do the talking, while you assess the people and the situation around you. When you're at ease, of course, you can talk the hind legs off a donkey. You are usually very smartly dressed, in an up-to-date manner with stylish and slightly unconventional clothing.

Virgo characteristics

This section can double up as a brief guide to Virgo as a Sun sign as well as a rising sign, so it provides a handy reference for you if you wish to check out someone's Sun sign as well as their rising sign. Do be a bit wary in the case of Virgo rising because there are quite a few differences between the Sun in Virgo and Virgo rising.

This is a contradictory and complicated sign to describe; the repressive childhood can leave a legacy of shyness and poor self-esteem which may never be overcome. Although there are others who, perhaps because they have several planets in less inhibited signs, can achieve a good deal of worldly success later in life. The earthiness of the sign makes you practical, capable and good with your hands. You may be an excellent gardener, decorator or a terrific cook. I have come across Virgo rising subjects whose daily life is spent in high-level business negotiations but whose private pastimes are cooking and gardening. The energies of this sign are directed to both the hands and the mind, therefore you bring craftsmanship to all your tasks and the orderliness of your mind suggests that you go about things in a logical and sensible manner. Your home and your workplace may be untidy but they are probably clean and fairly systematic.

You need a stable family environment, especially if you suffered from the usual Virgoan emotional poverty during your childhood. Many Virgo rising subjects marry and bring up children while they are quite young. You cope with early responsibility of this kind very well. If you are lucky with your choice of partner you will grow in confidence, going on to lead a happy, if rather ordinary, life. You take marriage seriously, and your desire to serve the needs of others suggests that you put a lot of effort into relationships. It may be hard for you to express affection openly because you find it easier to show your love by doing things for your family rather than by any show of sloppy sentimentality. As a parent, you may be fussy and inclined to worry too much about your children's health or with their behaviour, but your love for them is genuine and very generously given. Under the best of circumstances, you can put right the wrongs of your own childhood and become a truly successful relater. If you are not so lucky in your choice of partner, you will continue to suffer the kinds of injustices which you endured in your childhood.

Having harped on rather sanctimoniously about Virgoans' undoubted worth as caring and responsible family members, I will now bring us all back to earth. You are saved from being a complete stuffed-shirt or a self-righteous bore by your habit of unfaithfulness! Even though you are an exemplary person in most ways, you can be 'slippery' in personal relationships; but more of this in the 'relating' section.

Your generosity and kindness leads you to offer help to others, either directly by working in one of the caring professions, or on a spare-time basis. Virgo rising subjects can be found in the Scout movement, in nursing, as ambulance drivers, committee members and as astrological counsellors. You are an early riser and a hard and conscientious worker; you even take your spare time duties seriously. You can be surprisingly ambitious but you might find it difficult to progress if you bog yourself down with too much detail, worry too much about what other people think of you or allow your shyness to hold you back. Once you overcome these problems you can aim very high and your success is often aided by your intuitive understanding of the motives of others and a quick grasp of the political situation in your workplace.

You are hard on yourself, being very self-critical and if you find yourself misjudging a situation or coming out with an inappropriate remark, you may punish yourself silently for days afterwards. You also worry far too much about things which just aren't worth worrying about. If there were going to be a change in management at your workplace, you would worry yourself sick. Your dreams would be filled with sackings and applications to the social security office.

Virgoans are naturally rather secretive and are also subtle thinkers, therefore you can handle sensitive and confidential matters very well. Emotionally you are withdrawn. The Virgo rising child who lowered his eyes in silent shame when being harangued by an adult may later turn into a self-contained and secretive adult. If too much pain goes inwards, it will re-emerge later in nervous ailments or old-womanish fussiness. Even if you are well-adjusted to life you will have perfectionist habits somewhere along the line. Your own personal standards are high, you expect too much of yourself and sometimes also of others.

Many Virgoans are funny about food. You may have become a vegetarian years ago, long before it was fashionable or you may follow some kind of religion which prohibits normal eating. You may simply be choosy, only liking certain kinds of food, or foods which are cooked in a particular way. One Virgo rising friend of mine will eat almost anything – as long as it is cooked and prepared to gourmet standards!

Your faults are small but irritating for others to live with; for example, you may drive yourself and others to distraction by worrying needlessly about some small problem. The feminine/ earth aspects of Virgo certainly give you practicality but the sign's ruler, Mercury, makes you quick to change your mind and your moods, thereby making it hard for other people to understand you.

You need to spend time alone, to think and to relax your taut nerves. You may take up some sport or hobby because you think it will be 'good for you', but you soon become bored with it because you enjoy mental stimulation far more than the physical kind. You can sink into pettiness and fussy old-womanish ways if you are not careful. However, this will be alleviated if you have some fire influence on your birthchart.

The mid-heaven
This section and those which follow apply only to Virgo rising. The mid-heaven can show your aims and ambitions, therefore it can throw some light on your choice of career. In the case of

Virgo rising in UK latitudes, the mid-heaven covers the latter
part of Taurus and a good deal of Gemini. In southern Europe
and the United States, you will have a Taurus mid-heaven only
if your ascendant is in the first couple of degrees. The vast
majority of people born with Virgo rising have their mid-heaven
in Gemini.

Virgo/Taurus
The effect of having earth signs on both the ascendant and the
MC makes you practical, sensible and probably rather
materialistic and this need for security leads you to find work in
a safe and established trade. Both Virgo and Taurus are
interested in the growth and production of food, therefore you
could work as a farmer, market gardener, dietician or cook. The
building trade is another possibility, as is work connected with
buildings, such as fitting out, furnishing or dealing with
property. The insurance business is also possible.

Your outlook is traditional and your attitude to work and
money practical and sensible. Too much change, challenge and
excitement would unnerve you but a steady, ordinary and
reasonable job would suit you well. Virgo is concerned with
health and healing but Taurus can't stand blood and mess, so
the prevention of illness by diet and exercise might appeal more
than dealing directly with sick people. This combination
suggests a need for comfort at home and a good standard of
living. Your considerable ambition would be turned towards
providing this for yourself and your family. Taurus is associated
with music and Virgo with words, therefore, if your birthchart
has a creative slant, you could be drawn to the music or the
publishing trades.

Virgo/Gemini
This is the sign of the competent secretary, media researcher,
nurse or teacher. Both Virgo and Gemini are ruled by the planet
Mercury, therefore you are very interested in all forms of
communication; this might include teaching and studying,
telephone and telex work, writing and publishing, journalism or
driving. Your mind is active and you have a need to express
yourself but your shyness suggests that you are happier as a

backroom boy or girl than out in front of the public. The food and health connection could lead you to write on these subjects as well as to work in their fields. You might be interested in nutrition, medical research or methods of plant cultivation.

The Gemini factor could take you into journalism where your attention to detail and analytical mind would come in handy. There is a kind of intellectual detachment about you which suggests that you look deeply at whatever you are working on rather than taking anything on face value. Your strong desire to help others both directly and indirectly, could lead you into the counselling or medical fields, especially medical research. Communication in the form of travel and transport might attract you, therefore the travel trades, driving or vehicle maintenance could be good careers. Your meticulous and orderly mind could attract you to computing, systems analysis or accountancy. Other possibilities are electrical work or maintenance, electronics, radar, telecommunications or television and video engineering. Any kind of statistical work might appeal, as might research and analysis. Some Virgo rising subjects make very good historians.

The mid-heaven can sometimes denote the kind of person who attracts us or with whom we feel comfortable in day-to-day life. Therefore, you might find that you get on well, both at work and in your private life, with Taurus or Gemini types.

The descendant

The opposite point to the ascendant is the descendant or the cusp of the seventh house. Traditionally, this is supposed to show the kind of person to whom you are attracted. When Virgo is rising, the descendant is in Pisces and this nebulous sign may bring difficulties in relationships. You may attract people who are out of the ordinary or even somewhat peculiar. It seems as if this descendant is trying to compensate for your down-to-earth attitude to life by throwing a spanner in the works just where you least need one. You may find yourself attached to a partner who drinks or, worse still, is mentally unstable. To some extent it is your desire to help and to reform others which may land you in this pickle. You may fall for someone whose superficial appearance hides weakness, an inability to relate or even a cruel streak.

On the plus side, you could attract gentle, rather mystical types who want to care for and serve the needs of the family, just as you do. You seek kindness in a partner and will act kindly and charitably towards them. You can be happy with a partner who is musical, artistic and caring as long as they also pull their weight at work and at home. You can put up with a lot, just as long as your partner is basically decent and honest. You, yourself, can be decent and totally reliable in practical matters but potentially unfaithful sexually. Here we go again with those Virgoan contradictions.

Love, sex and relating – regardless of the descendant

This area of your life, as you have probably guessed, has all the appearance of a first-class minefield, especially when one looks at the contradictions in your own nature. You are shy, modest and possibly a touch fearful when it comes to sex. On the face of it, it might be better if you left this side of life until you were mature enough to cope with it – say around the age of 70; but that's not the way it happens. The chances are that your first encounter with sex came when you were in your teens – and your early teens at that! There could be any number of reasons for this. You could have been attracted, lulled or projected into a sexual relationship far too quickly. Your own desperate need for someone to provide you with some form of love and approval might have been the spur here. Some Virgoans trade sex for company, comfort and companionship. Oddly enough, considering the modesty and fastidiousness of this sign, you have a strong, needy and inventive sex-drive which, coupled with your curiosity, can lead you into all kinds of adventures. In short, despite all the repression, guilt and fear of making a fool of yourself, the enjoyment of lunch, love and lust creates a surprising metamorphosis in you.

You are experimental in bed and analytical afterwards; you may enjoy your private mental action-replays as much as you enjoyed the first-hand experience. Oddly enough, for such a responsible and family-minded sign, you are quite likely to be unfaithful in marriage. Why, I wonder? Possibly the need to experiment, compare and to analyse; the intellectual need to know what the world and the people in it are all about; or perhaps the need to keep a door open on all relationships and give yourself an impression of freedom even within a commitment. Maybe it's your way of getting back at a repressive partner or coping with a bad marriage. It seems that when you meet someone interesting you simply have to check them out; it is a form of the 'don't die wondering' syndrome! Your quiet, humorous and laid-back manner is charming and attractive to others, as is your quite genuine desire to please and, above all, to communicate.

Health

Your health is probably lousy. If it isn't, then you could suffer from hypochondria! Traditionally, your skin, bowels and nerves are weak spots but, in truth, you could have any ailment you desire. Like your Gemini-rising cousins, your nerves will let you down and can be guaranteed to plunge you into an illness whenever the going gets tough. Toothache, backache and inexplicable stomach pains are all possibilities, as are chronic ailments of all kinds. If you haven't had asthma or hay fever yet, you never know – this might be your 'lucky' year.

Here comes that contradiction again: Virgoans are *strong*; far stronger than their Leo or Libra neighbours, but they *need* a spell of bad health from time to time in order to switch off and rest.

Your sixth house is in Aquarius, so please also look at the health section on page 172.

CHAPTER 10

Libra Rising

We don't bother much about dress and
Manners in England, because as a
Nation we don't dress well and we've
No manners.

George Bernard Shaw, *You Never Can Tell*

A few words of explanation

A sign on the ascendant expresses itself in a different way from a
Sun sign; however some of the characteristics, even the
childhood experiences will apply if you have the Sun in Libra or
the seventh house. If your Moon is in Libra or the seventh
house, your emotions and reactions will have a Libran flavour. If
the ascendant is weak (see Chapter 1), the Libra overlay will not
be so noticeable. If the rest of the birthchart is very different

from the rising sign there could be a conflict within the personality. This is because the outer manner, the signals which are given out at first meeting by the subject, is very different from the main character which lies underneath. Another possibility is that the subject rejects all that his parents and teachers stood for and creates a life for himself very different from the one which he lived through as a child.

Remember that Libra is a cardinal sign which means that there is a limit to what you will put up with. It is also masculine, positive and airy in character, which suggests that you appear outgoing and enterprising and that you prefer to deal with the world from a mental or intellectual standpoint. This is a sign of long Ascension, so there are plenty of you around.

Early experiences

This sign on the ascendant denotes a good start in life. However there may be a few drawbacks even when this most pleasant sign is rising. Your parental home was probably comfortable, your parents kind and your relationship with childhood friends reasonable. As a small child, you were good looking, popular and charming and you managed to keep out of any real trouble both at home and at school. All in all, your childhood experiences were better than most, so what's the problem?

The problem is subtle, and it varies a little from one Libra rising subject to the next. Your parents may have left you to your own devices because they were busy. In some cases the father was a distant figure, he may have travelled away from home in connection with work or he may have walked away from the marriage and left the family; in many cases he actually died when the subject was very young. Sometimes the relationship with the father is quite good but the subject seems to be at odds with the mother. Whatever the actual situation may be, the feeling is one of distance and neglect. It may be that the subject and his parents don't share the same values or that they have natures which clash, although any clashing will be done quietly when this sign is rising. There are many Libra rising subjects who are lavished with guilt-induced 'goodies' by parents who neglect them.

In less difficult circumstances, you will have grown up being well cared for and well understood. Your sisters and brothers may have been less than impressed by your charm, and could have behaved in a jealous and spiteful manner towards you. You were probably a langorous child; lazy, slow-moving, quiet and well-behaved. If your parents were not too neglectful, they would have given you every opportunity to stretch your mind and encouraged you to do well at school. It is unlikely that a great deal of pressure was put on you to succeed but there was pressure to conform and not to make waves.

Being independent, even as a child, it is possible that your religious beliefs and political opinions have developed differently from those of your parents. Libra rising subjects don't usually come from a highly religious background but, oddly enough, their parents seem to have very strong political views. Belonging as you do to an independent-minded air sign, you would have listened to their opinions and then formed your own at a later stage in life. Although slow to do anything, and very slow to come to any kind of decision, you were quite able to think things out for yourself and to work out what you wanted to believe in.

You had, even as a child, a great desire to be surrounded by beauty. Your sense of taste and style is innate – it would have been hard for you to live with mess, dirt and disorder. The chances are that your parents' home was tasteful and attractive, and your own possessions clean and well cared for. You are not slovenly yourself and neither were your parents. You appreciate the arts, music and anything which is attractive and well thought out. You could have been artistically creative, especially if there are other forces on your birthchart to back this up. Librans have a natural kind of refinement. It is possible, even as a small child, that you assisted your parents in planning and working on a garden or in choosing the colour schemes for the house. This natural Libran taste can be useful to others. I usually ask my Moon-in-Libra son to choose household things for me, because his 'eye' is far better than mine.

Appearance
Where this is concerned, please take into consideration racial

factors and the rest of the birthchart. You are good looking, although not necessarily beautiful. Your features are refined, delicate and attractive. Even if you are plump, you will have a clear skin, beautiful eyes and a lovely smile. In white races, the skin is very fair and the eyes are large, widely set and often a pale luminous grey. You are probably a little below average height with a body which is long in proportion to your legs. Your posture is good and you move with a kind of liquid grace. Your choice of clothing may be conventional or outrageous but it will always be classy, expensive and in keeping with your personality. You like to keep your clothes for a long time and are prepared to spend money on dry-cleaning, therefore you tend to buy quality goods which will last.

Outer manner

You are charm personified. People take to you at once, because of your friendly approach and your genuine interest in what they have to say. Pleasant, humorous and gentle, you are easy to talk to and to get along with, at least on the surface. You enjoy a good old gossip but are rarely sarcastic or hurtful. Your manner of dealing with the world is reasonable, respectful, calm and businesslike, it is rarely brisk or officious. At work you appear to be capable, with an unhurried style which belies your ambition. Friends drift in and out of your life and though you may forget them for a while, you are always pleased to see them again when they reappear. Unfortunately you lack sincerity, and intuitive people spot this immediately.

Libra characteristics

This section can double up as a brief guide to Libra as a Sun sign *or* as a rising sign, so it can provide a handy reference if you want to check up on someone's Sun sign as well as their rising sign.

Lovely, laid-back Libra – yet another contradictory sign. The evidence from my questionnaires suggests that you didn't enjoy your childhood very much. It is possible that you were afraid of your father, while you may have harboured contempt for your mother. Children from all signs of the zodiac are chivvied by their parents and teachers into making efforts, and many a child is castigated for his or her sloth. ('Why are you sprawling in front of the telly when you've homework to do?') Librans seem to be blamed for this more than most. You have a great knack for switching off when asked to do something you don't fancy. You can work very hard, but this will be in fits and starts. You can make a concerted effort when pursuing some money-making scheme or when pursuing a debt, but you cannot keep up the pressure for long because at heart you are lazy.

Librans can be highly ambitious. Remember, this is a cardinal sign. You hate to miss a good opportunity; however your ambitions may not be immediately obvious to others. Many Librans put the minimum effort into their career while working hard at some outside interest. One example is a friend of mine who has served in the Territorial Army for many years without a break while moving around from one job to another. Many of you are musical, continuing to put time and effort into a musical hobby, even when other interests wane.

Your pleasant outer manner may hide contempt for others. It may also hide fear, inhibition and a well-concealed indifference to the needs of others. Some Libra rising subjects, however, are idealistic, truly hoping to make life fuller and better for other people by working in politics or for some worthy cause. You have one really tremendous virtue, and that is your common sense approach to problems. This, coupled with your marvellous ability to listen and give good sensible advice, easily outweighs all your vices. Your talent for listening and advising is terrific but you haven't got the strength, or the patience, to become permanently or heavily involved in the problems of others. You yourself need a listening ear from time to time as your confidence is fragile and you cannot always cope with life.

Libra rising subjects of both sexes are highly domesticated. You may be an excellent cook, a terrific do-it-yourselfer or an inspired antique collector. You may, indeed, be all three. You love your home and enjoy family life. The chances are that you will marry and have children while you are quite young. If you are fortunate in your choice of partner, your marriage will be a great success; however, if it doesn't work out, you will move on and look for someone else. You may be quite hard on your own children, demanding better behaviour and a higher standard of education than you, yourself, achieved. There may be a measure of over-compensation here against your own laissez-faire childhood. You are generous to your partner and also to your children. While it may be true that your children are chivvied to 'perform' well, they are unlikely to be kept short of anything which they need. You, yourself, need a good home, filled with the nicest things for yourself and your family.

As a rising sign even more than as a Sun sign, Libra is concerned with external appearances and the projection of an image. The image may vary from 'yuppy success story' to 'hip musician', but it is always 'cool' in every sense of the word. Confrontations are seen as being uncool and therefore avoided wherever possible. You tend to say what other people want to hear in order to be tactful. Female subjects can project a very feminine or a very sexy image which conceals a cool business head.

I would like to point out something which I have never seen recorded anywhere and that is your gift for spiritual healing. Maybe this is allied to your ability to listen and advise sympathetically. Maybe it has nothing at all to do with it; but I have come across many good healers who have Libra strongly placed in their birthchart. There is another side to the same coin which governs your superb arbitration talents, and that is your ability to argue a point to the bitter end. You may lose sight of reality while you are arguing and end up making absolutely no sense at all but you will win by sheer persistence.

Mid-heaven

This section and those which follow apply only to Libra rising and not to Sun in Libra. The mid-heaven shows the subject's aims and ambitions, his public standing and his attitude to work outside the home. In the case of births in the UK and Europe, most Libra rising subjects have their mid-heaven in Cancer. However those whose ascendant is in the latter part of the sign will have their MC in Leo. For births in the south of Europe and in the United States, almost the whole of this rising sign will have the MC in Cancer and only those with the ascendant in the last few degrees in Libra will have their MC in Leo.

Libra/Cancer

This combination can make for a shrewd businessman or woman. You take your time before committing yourself to anything, carefully weighing up the pros and cons. The Cancerian mid-heaven can lead to an interest in antiques, coin collecting or Egyptology. This may sound peculiar, but it is worth remembering that Cancer is concerned with the past and you may wish to incorporate objects or ideas from the past into your daily life.

Libra, being an air sign, is interested in communicating, keeping up-to-date and being out among people, while Cancer likes to work quietly for himself. This apparent contradiction can be overcome by either doing your own thing inside a large organization or by doing your own thing in some kind of loose association with others. One instance which demonstrates this is a friend of mine who runs a small accountancy business from home, thereby combining her need for autonomy and privacy with her need to communicate with the world at large. Cancer, being a caring sign, can suggest a nursing or counselling career. You may enjoy teaching very young children either in a school or in a Sunday school. This combination is an excellent one for a career in politics, or a quasi-political career such as Trades Union negotiator.

Oddly enough, I have come across a number of electricians and electrical engineers with this rising sign. Maybe the Cancerian MC makes you want to improve people's home and business premises, or maybe it's the presence of air on the ascendant which gives you an affinity to electrical or magnetic forces. Libra is associated with the planet Venus, and this gives you a strong interest in beauty in all its forms, so you may consider working in the field of fashion, cosmetics and design. You may exploit your flair for interior design commercially.

Libra/Leo

This combination suggests a need to leave your mark on the world. You may be attracted to a job which offers you a chance to shine or to use your dramatic flair in some way. The Leo MC seeks the limelight while the Libran ascendant wants to advise others, therefore a position such as a theatrical agent, recruitment consultant or an agony aunt might appeal. Both Leo and Libra are creative signs, so you may choose to work in the fields of design, fashion, jewellery, cosmetics or interior design. Your designs would be both tasteful and opulent.

This combination suggests work in an advisory capacity as, for example, a solicitor, counsellor, consultant, doctor or hypnotherapist. Medical and healing work often appeals to people who have this combination, probably because with a Leo MC so much of the first house is in medically-minded Scorpio. The drawback to this combination is that both the MC and the rising signs denote laziness, so you may have difficulty in finishing the projects which you start.

The mid-heaven can indicate the type of person to whom you are attracted, both as a personal and a business partner, therefore you could have an affinity with Cancer or Leo types.

The descendant

The opposite point to the ascendant is the descendant or the cusp of the seventh house. Traditionally this is supposed to show the kind of person to whom you are attracted. When Libra is rising, the descendant is in Aries, therefore the enthusiasm and enterprise of Aries types may well attract you. I have noticed that many Librans do actually marry Arians but this union is apt to frustrate both parties because the Arian becomes bored with the Libran's slow, calculating outlook, while the Libran becomes tired of the Arian's childishness. Libra may also object to the Arian's dictatorial manner.

Librans need a partner who enjoys work. You are happy to have them work alongside you, as long as they don't try to make your decisions for you. The cardinal quality of the signs on your ascendant and descendant suggest that you must lead, albeit slowly, rather than follow. You require a fairly calm partner who has a strongly confident centre to his or her personality because you have a habit of taking your everyday frustrations out on your nearest and dearest, or ignoring them when you're in a bad mood.

A clingy, unreasonable or jealous partner is no good for you, as you detest being pinned down or having to account for your movements. Oddly enough, you succeed in one situation where many others fail, and that is in the area of second marriages. You do not trouble yourself to argue with step-children or ex-wives or husbands, preferring to keep the peace if at all possible. Inside your own one-to-one relationship you may be far from peaceful, but to those on the periphery you appear to be decent and reasonable. If you find yourself drawn into a wider family group, you manage very well because you enjoy the fun of family life and all the extra opportunities for conversation and advice-giving. One point which must be made is that you like to experiment with relationships; therefore, you may find commitment and faithfulness impossible.

Love, sex and relating – regardless of the descendant

Despite your cool outer image, relating is never a cool business for you. Somewhere along the line you will fall in love and when this happens you will fall hard. You may not show your feelings to the world but they are strong and deep nevertheless. If you are let down and hurt by this experience you hide your feelings, but they go down deeper than anyone can guess and it is unlikely that you will ever allow yourself to be placed in that situation again. This is a shame because the next person who comes along may be far more worthy of your love, but by then it is too late. Once you have been burned you never place your hand in the fire again.

When you do feel intensely about your partner, your lovemaking can reach magical proportions and even when this is not the case you are a notably good lover. Libra is a hedonistic sign which enjoys any kind of sensual experience, good food, good music and, of course, good sex. You take the trouble to make sure your partner enjoys the experience as much as you yourself and your sensual laziness ensures that you take your time over the process.

There are two further comments which I would like to make about this sign. The first is that you don't like to make love in scruffy or uncomfortable surroundings and the second is that,

much as you enjoy sex, you may not want to indulge yourself
very often. You may prefer great sex once a month to 'so-so sex
three times a week!

Health
Traditionally, the Libran problem areas are the bladder and the
soft organs of the stomach. Your liver and pancreas may be
weak, so you should limit your alcohol intake and avoid too
much sweet food. You could have a weight problem but your
natural vanity might urge you to take action when you realize
that you are beginning to look tubby. Libra rules the motor
development of the nervous system and, therefore, can be
involved with rheumatic or nervous problems, particularly in the
spinal column.

Your sixth house is in Pisces, so please also look at the health
section on page 185.

CHAPTER 11

Scorpio Rising

Give me more Love, or more Disdain;
the Torrid, or the Frozen Zone
Bring equal ease unto my paine:
The Temperate affords me none:
Either extreme, of Love or Hate,
Is sweeter than a calme estate.

Thomas Carew *Mediocrity in Love
Rejected*

A few words of explanation
A sign on the ascendant expresses itself in a different way from
the Sun sign. However, some of the characteristics, even the
childhood experiences will apply if you have the Sun in Scorpio
or in the eighth house. There will be some of these character-

istics present if you have Mars or Pluto in Scorpio or in the eighth house. If your Moon is in Scorpio, your emotions will have a Scorpionic flavour. If the ascendant is weak (see Chapter 1), the Scorpio overlay will not be so noticeable. If the rest of the birthchart is very different from the rising sign there could be a conflict within the personality. This is because the outer manner, the signals which are given out at first meeting by the subject, is very different from the main character which lies underneath. Another possibility is that the subject rejects all that his parents, parent figures and teachers stood for, and creates a life for himself which is very different from the one which they envisaged for him, or the one which he lived through as a child.

Remember that this is a fixed sign, which implies the ability to stay with a situation and see it through. It is also a water sign, which suggests deep emotions which have a bearing on the subject's behaviour. This is also a sign of long ascension, so there should be plenty of you around.

Early experiences
Scorpio is such an intense sign that one could be forgiven for assuming that this must indicate a particularly difficult childhood. The fact is that there is a wide spectrum of childhood experiences to be found amongst the Scorpio population. Some have truly horrifying childhood experiences, while others seem to have been quite happy. Many Scorpio rising children are naturally cautious and rather withdrawn; they hide their emotions behind a poker face or a blank stare. This makes them hard to read and hard to get close to, which may cut them off from others. If you are a Scorpio rising subject who was ignored as a child, I suggest that you think back to the way *you* behaved and reacted towards others. Did you make any attempt to reach out and touch people? Did you take any interest in their needs or did you simply hide behind your mask, living inside your own head, interested only in your own dreams and desires? This is a difficult situation to explain because there is a chicken and egg aspect here which could have arisen either from a genuine inability to relate to one or more members of your family, or simply because your closed-in manner caused them to

withdraw from you. In some cases, there clearly *was* a problem and I shall try to demonstrate some of the difficulties which you may have encountered. I apologize if this explanation is a bit of a list but there are many possibilities.

At the very worst end of the spectrum, some Scorpio rising children are genuinely afraid of one or both of their parents. Some of you feared other relatives or family friends with whom you had to deal. There may, for example, have been an uncle who stood too close to you or a lodger who touched you inappropriately. Even if there was nothing obviously wrong, you may have had an awareness of danger and a sense that all was not as it should have been. Remember that Scorpio is associated with sex, and it is not all that uncommon for children to be taken advantage of. Even if nothing untoward happened, you could have been aware of undercurrents which should not have been present.

Some of you grew up in the kind of home where the father was violent, unpredictable and frequently drunk, while mother was an ineffectual victim. Others had impossible levels of achievement demanded of them by an ambitious mother who lived through her children. Whatever the circumstances, you learned early to keep your feelings under control and never allow your face to betray the thoughts which were running around in your head. This retreat behind the mask, the closed-face withdrawal, is the classic benchmark of this rising sign. One such subject confided to a friend of mine that, when she was nine years old, her truly dreadful, drunken, bully of a father died and she had to make an effort to hide her lack of grief. She says that only on rare occasions since has she ever allowed anyone to know how she felt. In some cases, a parent dies and the problem is caused by another adult.

Another possibility is that you developed different values and priorities from the rest of your family and decided that it would be better to keep these quiet. These differing values could have consisted of almost anything; perhaps your parents sought a pedestrian way of life, a humdrum existence, while you yearned for something more exciting and more meaningful. I have come across Scorpio rising subjects who left their parental home at the first opportunity because it was boring and stultifying, mentally and physically cramped, and financially or academically impoverished.

In the years after the Second World War and up to 1960, every young man between the ages of about 18 and 20 had to spend some time in the forces. This took them away from their families and made them see life from a different angle, just at the moment when they were developing into individual adults. For many Scorpio rising youngsters this was a heaven-sent opportunity to get away from home and see something of the world. Girls with this rising sign often 'escaped' into an early marriage in order to have a home and a life of their own. How these youngsters progressed after leaving home depended in part upon their natures and also on the luck of the draw.

There are Scorpionic subjects who got on famously with their families while they were small, only to experience difficulties as they began to grow up and develop ideas of their own. In this case, puberty became a nightmare for all concerned, with the child leaving, or being ejected from the home some time during his teens. Other Scorpio rising subjects have a great time at home with the family but experience problems at school. Sometimes these problems are associated with a particular stage of their schooling, while other Scorpios never seem to get it together where education is concerned. There are Scorpio rising subjects who loved school, and used it as an escape from a mundane or claustrophobic home atmosphere.

I would like to offer the story of my friends, Gillian and Anna, as an example of the subtle difficulties which are associated with this sign on the ascendant. Gillian and Anna are sisters who were born about a year apart. Gill, who was my own special friend, was the elder. Gill was born with her Sun in Gemini and Scorpio on the ascendant, while Anna, the more outgoing of the two girls, had her Sun in Sagittarius but also had Scorpio rising. There had been another much older sister called Tracy who, during the 1950s, met a GI, married him, and emigrated to the United States. I always had a feeling that Tracy was not a natural full sister to the two girls but I have never asked them about this.

Gill and Anna's parents occupied the downstairs part of an old house. Mr Keane, their father, was to my 12 year old eyes, an old man. He had some kind of night-watchman's job and his spare time was spent making their scrap of London-clay-plus-filth front garden into an absolute picture. I have never in all my life seen dahlias like those which Mr Keane so devotedly grew. In bad weather he sat in front of their kitchen boiler fire, sharing the space with strings of washing and reading the *Daily Mirror*. About once every hour he would grunt something incomprehensible through his couple of remaining teeth. I cannot remember him speaking to me or even to the girls very much except to tell them to shut up if they were making too much noise, but apparently (so they later told me) the girls loved him.

Mrs Keane, on the other hand, was a lovely woman. Totally useless in a way many women were in those days, she suffered from angina and agoraphobia and never left the house. To me, growing up in a family where everyone around me died, walked off or ran exciting businesses elsewhere, Mrs Keane's constant presence represented a rare kind of luxury. Needless to say, there was hardly a penny to spare but Mrs K's kettle was always on, and she was always ready for a chat and always interested, in a totally positive way, in everything that we three girls did. She joined in on wet days when we drew or played cards, helping to find string, glue and anything else that we needed for our games. She was a warm, permanent centre to our lives but, in the eyes of the world and, of course, in the eyes of the two growing girls, she appeared far too slow and uninspiring.

Gill and Anna looked increasingly outwards to a world where fun, money, men and the unexpected awaited. Soon after they left school they moved out. The first to go was Gill, who took a live-in job in Cornwall where she became part servant and part trainee horse rider and instructor. She met and married a local man and went on to have a daughter, Rachael. The marriage was a disaster and for a while Gill became a carbon copy of her mother: large, ill and confined to her Cornish home; but now I'm glad to say that she is at work and enjoying her life.

Anna got engaged and, shortly afterwards, became pregnant at the age of 17. The guy who was to be her escape route refused to marry her but, before the baby was born, she met and married Bill, a bus driver, and moved out to a flat a few miles away. Anna has had a couple of husbands since Bill and also several more children, a couple of whom are severely handicapped (more of this interesting phenomenon later). Anna became a nurse and, as far as I know, is now living with yet another guy, working and probably enjoying life a bit more now that her family are at last growing up.

As you can see, neither of these girls' lives are especially remarkable, but they do reflect the Scorpionic disenchantment with childhood and the need to get away at any price. I seriously urge any Scorpio rising youngster who is reading this book to think and plan for your future rather than to run directly towards the first available option, in case the price of escape proves to be just that bit too high. Incidentally, neither Gill nor Anna liked school very much. Gill, in particular, hated her junior school and only learned to read and write properly when she and I were about 12 or 13 years old and needless to say it was I who taught her. I still think back to those two beautiful and imaginative girls whose lives seemed to have been blighted by their lack of sensible planning and their sheer bad luck.

As far as schooling is concerned, I have come across Scorpio rising subjects who were very successful, leaving their contemporaries behind as a result. Some subjects are gifted artists and musicians which, once again, seems to separate them from their contemporaries. Yet others educate themselves out of their social class or have sexual needs which don't fit in with their background. It is this separateness which is at the heart of this rising sign. Sometimes, this separateness is caused by nothing more than the hawk-eyed glare or the flat-faced blank stare emanating from these children's faces which keeps people at a distance and ensures their encapsulation within their own persona.

Finally, back to a subject which I touched upon when talking about Anna. This rising sign is frequently involved with handicaps of one kind or another. I have come across too many instances for it to be mere coincidence. There are Scorpio rising subjects who are mentally or physically handicapped and therefore unable to get around easily or to communicate easily. Some people start out normally enough but by accident, disease or even by their choice of lifestyle, become prevented in some way from living a full life. Others bring up handicapped children themselves. It seems that if Scorpio is strongly shown on a birthchart some connection with helplessness and restriction is inevitable.

Jealousy is very much associated with Scorpio. You may attract envy from others, especially later in life but it is usually you who has to suffer the fires of this most awful and most useless emotion, especially while you are young. Others around you seem to have so much more than you, either in terms of possessions or in their appearance and their status within the group. It is not uncommon for you to burn with jealousy over a luckier or more gifted brother or sister. My Scorpio rising mother cheerfully admits that she loathed her younger sister because she had good looks, the love of their mother and was the recipient of every opportunity that could be mustered for her. My mother, being the elder sister, was sent out to work so that Anne, her younger sister, could have dancing lessons. Many years later, after many ups and downs, Anne, widowed and alone, lost her mind and ended her life in an institution, while my mother, happily married to my lovely step-father is still enjoying a full working and social life at the age of 81! This is typical of the sign, so if you feel that everyone around you is a winner and that you are always cast as the loser, just wait – the tables will surely turn.

Appearance

Taking into account racial and other astrological factors, you are probably shorter than average, broad, stocky and inclined to put on weight easily. Your colouring is sallow and your hair mid to dark brown. Your hair is one of your best features as it is often thick, springy and abundant, keeping its good looks throughout your life. Your hands and feet are small and neat and your movements are economical and quite graceful. You have a lovely smile which lights up your whole face but you have to know someone a little before you favour them with one of your lovely grins. You are light on your feet and a naturally good dancer but as you get older you have to guard against too much sitting about, as you will then begin to gain weight very quickly. Your best feature, a truly hidden asset, is your voice. This is low, quiet but oddly captivating. It commands respect and is a valuable asset to your sexual armoury.

There can be great variations in the appearance of Scorpio rising subjects but one thing is certain, you are not what the computer buffs calls 'WYSIWYG'. This high-tech term stands for 'what you see is what you get' and, in your case, what we see is definitely *not* what is going on behind your face. Some of you have a strangely flat-faced appearance with broad cheekbones and plenty of width across the eyes. This kind of face may lack expression which helps you to hide your feelings. Other Scorpio rising subjects have a terrifying hawk-like appearance which can be terribly off-putting on first meeting, especially to those with a nervous disposition. To tell you the truth, the hunter-harrier type scares me to death! This too, however, is a disguise which more than adequately conceals a soft heart. Other subjects are extremely good-looking with well defined features and strong bones.

All Scorpio rising subjects have a magnetic appearance but the handsome, dangerous, hypnotic variety of either sex is absolutely irresistible. I have no idea of the birth data but I wouldn't be surprised if the late James Mason, the film actor, had been a Scorpio rising subject – those melting eyes, that magnetic voice, wow! My mother has her Sun on the Scorpio/Libra cusp and also has a Scorpio ascendant. She is a terrifying individual, even now at the age of 81, very athletic, with all her brains intact and a razor-sharp tongue still in full working order. However, like the vast majority of Scorpio rising subjects her appearance hides a soft centre and a deep fund of generosity. Whether you love them or hate them, you cannot overlook a Scorpio rising subject.

Outer manner
Most people who have this rising sign are charming, fascinating and interesting to listen to. As a Scorpio rising subject, you

probably have some special ability or interest which makes you stand out from other people in some way. This slight studiousness, coupled with your diffidence, makes you appear clever and mysterious. You don't push yourself forward in social situations, being most relaxed when working on your own particular hobbies. It is always a joy to sit quietly and listen to you when you relax and open out. Your company is so good that time spent with you goes by quickly.

There are some Scorpio rising types who are thoroughly off-putting on first acquaintance, being sharp and forbidding, critical, offensive and rather frightening, but I have found that if I allow myself to slide behind the unpleasant mask there is always a fascinating person tucked safely away around the back of it. You are curious about the motives and behaviour of other people and may tend to put total strangers under interrogation, but even this unnerving trait is far preferable to the type of person who is terminally self-absorbed.

Scorpio characteristics

This section can double up as a brief guide to Scorpio as a Sun sign or as a rising sign, so it can provide a handy reference if you want to check up on someone's Sun sign, as well as their rising sign.

Scorpios are given a notoriously bad press in most astrology books, being written off as drunken sex maniacs with violent tendencies on the one hand, or the kind of mesmeric bodice-rippers so beloved of women's pulp fiction on the other. ('He caught her fragile body within the tensile strength of his muscular arms, the fluttering of her heart as she shivered against his chest meant nought to him as he brought his cruel mouth hard down upon her softly tremulous lips' . . .) The disappointing fact is that the majority of you are quiet, hard-working, reliable people, good to your families and kind to animals. However there is a powerful side to your nature, an ability to construct, destroy and reconstruct which sets itself into motion when your life begins to go wrong.

Your likes and dislikes are strongly felt. There are no half measures for you, no compromise and no response to coercion other than outright fury. When you approve of something or somebody it goes all the way, whilst no amount of mitigating circumstances will make you bend towards those whom you consider beneath contempt. A very simple example of this phenomenon in action is that of Tony, a Sun in Scorpio guy who cheerfully admits that he dislikes animals. Who but a Scorpio could admit to disliking animals? He even professes to enjoy the sight of spring lambs gambolling around in his freezer. This kind of remark is calculated to shock, and doesn't have to be taken too literally.

You certainly take your likes and dislikes to extremes. You may drink like a fish or be totally abstemious, you may spend money as if it were going out of fashion or use your purse so infrequently that moth larvae reside in it! Whatever your beliefs or values, you would rather lose a job, a lover or £1,000 in cash than change them.

At work, you either remain in a comfortable job which allows you to feel that you belong or you move upwards to become the head of a concern. Many of you run your own businesses, though freelance consultancy work might be too insecure for you. You are quite demanding when in a position of authority but rarely unpleasant or unreasonable (Montgomery of Alamein being a notable exception). You have the uncanny knack of commanding respect from junior employees and they usually continue to work for you over the years. Demanding you may be, but you don't change the rules from one day to the next, so people who work for you always know where they stand and what is expected of them. You, yourself, cannot abide the kind of boss who moves goal posts; you need to know what your duties are and to be left in peace to carry them out. Most of all, you hate being criticized.

Being a water sign you have a long memory. On a practical level this helps you amass and retain data in connection with your job. On a less practical side, you remember those who are good to you and never forget those who hurt or insult you. You remember birthdays, dates, times, places and the gossip and unwise confessions which the unwary let slip into your ears.

Your powers of endurance are incredible, and your health is

usually excellent. However, if you *do* fall ill, it is likely to be sudden and dramatic. Your powers of recovery are equally dramatic. You can put up with more hard work, discomfort and exhaustion than any three other signs combined. When you overwork, you may look as if you are coping calmly, but the truth is that you switch to a kind of overdrive facility which consists of determination, stretched nerves and tension. When this happens you may vent your tense feelings on your nearest and dearest. You can be co-operative when you feel like it, but you dislike being taken for granted. You may be helpful on occasion but this does not guarantee that you will be so all the time, and you despise what you see as weakness in others.

Remember that this is a water sign which, despite its fixed quality, denotes moodiness. Scorpios are proud, so your personal standards of behaviour are very high. You don't care much for personal criticism and you dislike jokes which are made at your expense. You can just about accept constructive criticism but are mortally offended by any kind of personal attack. The long Scorpio memory is attached to an ability to keep secrets, a quality which makes you a good choice for any kind of confidential work. Where your personal life is concerned you reveal little. You may appear quite open, even highly opinionated but your real feelings are tucked well away from view. If you find yourself in what you deem to be any kind of challenging or threatening situation, you can be very hostile.

Although this is not a notably intellectual sign, your curiosity about the world gives you a thirst for knowledge. You make sure that you are well-informed on a general level, street-wise even, but you probably have a special interest which holds your attention year after year. Some Scorpios are wonderful amateur historians, others are linguists, while yet others have a great love and knowledge of the natural world. You love to stretch your body so many of you are athletic or interested in dancing or swimming. You tend to keep these interests going throughout life. If other aspects of your chart back this up, you may have a lifelong interest in military matters and be very knowledgeable about military history.

Your need to delve into things can be expressed in a very

personal way. You may look through other people's cupboards out of curiosity. Recycling is another Scorpio passion. Like your fellow water sign of Cancer, you prefer articles which have been used before to new ones. 'Waste not, want not' is your watchword; jumble sales and the local Oxfam shop are your spiritual home. Your curious attachment to death may have begun in childhood where you became aware, as a result of the death of someone around you, that life can be nasty, brutish and short.

Your loyalty to your friends and family is intense and you would never abandon an elderly parent or a needy child. Even a wayward spouse is taken care of, although you would probably switch off from them on an emotional level. You don't run away from problems, indeed, you may hang on to bad situations long after they should be abandoned. You are reliable and dependable, very caring and often self-sacrifical with regard to your family and, despite the fact that you yourself are usually robust, you are patient with those who are sick. You are less than patient when you, yourself, are sick, as you either consider it to be an unacceptable sign of personal weakness or an unnecessary interruption to your daily life. Yes, it's true that Scorpios can be cruel, destructive, self-destructive, moody and totally impossible at times, but you prefer to give comfort, affection, love, and care, rather than to dish out pain to those you love. It is worth remembering that you may have been short-changed in terms of physical affection in childhood and you welcome the opportunity to give and receive cuddles and love when grown up. The main thing to remember when this sign is rising is that the outer personality, the messages which are given out at first meeting, is a mask under which there is, modified, of course, by the rest of the chart, a kindly loving person who wishes to leave this world a better place than he found it.

The mid-heaven
This section and those which follow apply only to Scorpio rising. The mid-heaven shows your aims and ambitions, therefore it can throw some light on your choice of career. In the case of Scorpio rising in the UK and similar northerly latitudes, the MC

is almost equally split between Leo and Virgo. In the USA and southern Europe about two thirds of the MC will be in Leo, with the remainder in Virgo. Either MC will make the subject cautiously ambitious but the drive to achieve will be directed differently.

Scorpio/Leo

These are both fixed signs which denote that the subject finds it hard to adapt to change. If you lose your job or suffer any type of setback which calls for a close look at your situation and your potential, you would view it as a tragedy rather than as a challenge. You would also harbour a deep and abiding resentment for the person or organization who placed you in such a position. However, your tremendous reserves of courage and energy would ensure that you didn't wallow in misery for long.

The fixed nature of this sign makes you reliable and efficient. There is a Scorpio motto which goes 'if you are going to do a job, then for goodness sake do it properly'. You are thorough and painstaking and you hate to be rushed and hassled whilst you are working. The Leo MC gives you a desire for status and glamour, while the Scorpio ascendant adds caution, tenacity and independence, therefore you head slowly towards the top, stamping your personal style upon your surroundings as you go.

You may be found running a business or at the head of a governmental department; you are also able to work alone on creative projects. This Scorpio/Leo combination could denote a winning athlete or a top psychiatrist. Acting is a possibility because here you can use the Leo MC to project emotion and to draw attention to yourself, without the risk of jeopardizing your well-protected persona. Scorpios frequently love music, of both the classical and the pop variety; Leos are also very 'into' music, therefore you could choose to work in the field of music-making, promotion or sales. Musical instruments and the computers and electronics which are nowadays associated with the making of music may interest you as well. As you can see, your career possibilities are diverse; they may include banking, teaching, coal or diamond mining. Many of you are fond of children and will either go into full-time teaching or, and this is more likely, spend some of your spare time scouting, guiding or something similar.

Many Scorpios are drawn to a military career. This gives you the company of people who didn't know you as a child, offering you a fresh start in life so that you can put the pain of your childhood behind you for good. The armed services provide opportunities for travel and sport, plus the opportunity to develop your natural interest in the vehicles and weapons of war. Remember that, before the discovery of the planet Pluto, Scorpio was said to be ruled by Mars, the god of war. Being especially drawn to the sea, you could join the navy or possibly the merchant marines. One Scorpio rising subject of my acquaintance left her awful childhood behind by taking a job on a cruise liner.

Many of you find your way into the police force, this being a job for which you are supremely fitted. You work well within a team and can command the respect of your comrades. Your investigative powers and natural mistrust of fellow humans stands you in good stead here, while your physical strength and well trained body enable you to enjoy exercise and combat. Many Scorpios are drawn to the world of the military and the para-military, just as many more are drawn to the world of medicine and para-medicine. These careers can be viewed as being useful to the community at large, offering aid and protection to the weak, and thus allowing you to express the 'knight in shining armour' aspects of your personality.

Scorpio/Virgo

This combination should lead you towards a medical career, or at least towards a strong interest in all aspects of mental and physical healing. The Scorpio/Virgo combination includes surgeons, doctors, herbalists, spiritual healers and psychiatrists. There is a desire to help humanity and at the same time a fascination with human and animal biology and perhaps even with mental and physical pain. The modest and retiring nature of this combination leads you to choose a job which allows you to stay in the background, therefore you would make a good civil servant, secretary and social worker. You could choose to work in the food or the clothing industry, or even in the trade of butchery. This is partly because Virgo is associated with food and clothing (Scorpio with knives and meat) but also because these jobs supply basic needs to the public. This need to do something which is useful to the public and which is helpful in an impersonal way stems from the same root as the 'knight in shining armour' image which I mentioned a while ago.

Oddly enough you may do well in the world of acting or dancing, as these are jobs which offer opportunities for safe self-expression and which bring influences to bear upon the public while giving pleasure. Spiritual healing might be an attractive interest. You could also be attracted to the use of alternative medicines and therapies; hypnotism is an especially common Scorpio interest. Religion also fascinates you, but the remainder of the chart will determine whether this takes you into the world of the 'respectable' churches, or the wider holistic philosophies of the New Age. It is worth bearing in mind that a late Scorpio ascendant puts a good deal of the first house into the religious and philosophical sign of Sagittarius.

General comments

Don't be too cut and dried with these MCs. The Scorpio/Leo person may be medically-minded while the Scorpio/Virgo person may be the one who runs away to sea. Just bear in mind that this ascendant needs to work and live close to the heart of life and death or at the creative heart of an important project. What you do should *matter*; it should leave its mark on the world and allow you to feel as if you count for something. It is also worth remembering that Scorpio is associated with sex, therefore rape crisis counselling may appeal to you, as might gynaecology – I guess even pornography might appeal, but if you were going to make films which were both artistic and successful, you would need a well placed Neptune in your birthchart!

The mid-heaven can sometimes indicate the type of person to whom you are attracted both as working partners and as lovers, so you might find yourself most comfortable alongside Leo and Virgo people.

The descendant
The opposite point to the ascendant is the descendant or the cusp of the seventh house. Traditionally, this is supposed to show the kind of person to whom you are attracted. In this case the seventh house cusp is in Taurus. When you find the right partner you settle down to a long-lived and very affectionate relationship, but even this relationship is not without fireworks. It is also worth noting that your most successful relationship is likely to be a second marriage (rather than a first one), coming along when you have learned a bit about living with others. You may 'try out' two quite different types of marriage, one with a sexy firebrand and another with a gentle uncritical homemaker. Assuming that your marriage is a success, you would enjoy becoming a parent, although you may have some unrealistic ideas of what it means to bring up children. It is worth remembering that your fifth house, the one which is concerned with children, is in the illusory and delusory sign of Pisces. If your partner were the Taurean type, you would share an appreciation of music and the sensual joys of good food and good sex. However, trouble could arise from the tendency for both of you to have powerful and destructive tempers.

To be honest, this sign does not carry the best auguries for happy relationships although, if you are not too uncompromising in outlook and the rest of your chart includes some lighter factors, they can work out very well. You take commitments seriously and that is an advantage.

Love, sex and relating – regardless of the descendant
There is no easy description for this. It would be all too easy to fall back on the 'sexy, passionate' image which is the usual theory regarding your sign, but I'm not so sure about this. Scorpio rising subjects can be extremely sexy, using sex as an outlet for bottled-up feelings, as a means to control and dominate a partner or as a form of reassurance. You can use sex to convince yourself that someone loves you, deluding yourself that just because they respond bodily to your efforts, they can't fail to be yours in mind and soul as well. You can use sex to prove that you count or even that you exist and, of course, also

for the sheer bloody pleasure of it.

Your patience, endurance and natural desire to give and receive would suggest that you do make an exceptional lover. You're not afraid to experiment, and nor are you easily disgusted, therefore your inhibitions should be few, if any. However, having said all this, I absolutely must point out that Scorpio is such an all-or-nothing sign that some of you are totally uninterested in sex. Some of you may be impotent, while others may be uncertain about your sexuality, while some of you are only interested in sex on a few very rare occasions (anniversaries and similar events). You may choose to remain celibate for religious reasons, or because you wish to save your strength for the athletic field or the boxing ring; yet others of you are fastidious and highly inhibited. Some Scorpios are genuinely terrified of the whole business or just plain umimpressed by it and therefore totally uninterested! As far as relating is concerned, this could go in a variety of directions.

There is a fabulous Sun sign astrology book called *The New Astrology*, written by Poppe Folly. This comically ironic book has this very apt comment in its Scorpio section: 'The casual violence of your successful marriages may appall everyone else, and terrify your children: attacks on your spouse they construe as attacks on themselves. This is why the little things sit at the top of the stairs rocking with horror when they hear you fighting through the night'. True! true! If a Scorpio rising woman marries a man who insists on leaving her at home with small children, too little housekeeping money and a blank refusal to share her burdens or treat her with a modicum of respect, then he is in for a nasty shock. Maybe his mother could be relied upon to lie down under this kind of treatment but his *wife* certainly will not. Violence can arise through jealousy or a fear of abandonment and oddly enough it is not necessarily the Scorpio who is the perpetrator of the violence! The Scorpio could himself be a prey to someone else's unreasonable feelings of possessiveness and jealousy. If you, as a Scorpio, feel threatened or maltreated you could enter into a war of attrition with your partner which could be carried on for years. This kind of relationship needs two warriors to keep it going, it won't work if your partner switches off or walks out.

Very few Scorpios can take criticism. You may take offence even at the most helpful, well-meant and constructive criticism. However you can be an expert at dishing it out. You quickly learn just which of your partner's buttons to push and won't be able to resist winding him up when he is feeling unwell or emotionally vulnerable. Scorpios need a lot of standing up to.

This list of disastrous relationship scenarios is no more than a list of possibilities. There are plenty of good husbands and wives with this sign rising. Many male Scorpios marry large, motherly women. You need affection, reassurance and a feeling of continuity. You appreciate acceptance, even by your spouse's family and you benefit greatly from a wise partner who encourages you to open out and express yourself. If you have the kind of partner who includes you in the mainstream of their life, who genuinely respects your opinions and wants your company, you are the best, the most loyal and hardworking mate in the whole zodiac.

I would like to point out a couple of curious facts relating to the area of children and childbirth. There is often something wrong here. A Scorpio rising woman will often bear at least one child out of wedlock, or she will marry a man who isn't the father of her child. Many of you leave the business of parenthood until relatively late in life and then only have one child. Scorpio mothers are often abandoned by their child's father or left to cope alone. Sometimes your resentment of this situation will be taken out on your children or, alternatively, you could push your children to obtain both the material goods and the status which you were never given the opportunity to have. This can be a very uneasy relationship in some cases, whilst in others, the lone chick and its mother cling together in a mutual outpouring of reciprocal love and affection.

Some astrology books note that Sun in Scorpio subjects are born at the time of a death in the family. My Solar Scorpio husband's elder brother died of complications from measles three months before my husband was born. I don't know whether this thought is relevant to Scorpio rising – perhaps you would like to do some research of your own on this one. One final comment here which neatly takes us forward into the health section, is that there are often problems associated with giving birth.

Health

The sexual organs may cause trouble. We have already mentioned childbirth, but other womb and related areas can present problems, while the male organs may suffer hernias and prostate gland difficulties. Vasectomies can go wrong on the one hand, or there may be something wrong with the sperm count. Scorpios are very healthy as a rule, but you can become sick very quickly and very dramatically from time to time. When this happens you instantly become an excellent patient (at least as far as the doctors and hospital are concerned). You respond to treatment and soon forget that you were ever very ill. Heart trouble is surprisingly common, as are stomach ulcers, or the less dramatic but equally uncomfortable ailment of acidity in the stomach. These illnesses result from your usual state of unreleased stress and tension. Meditation would be of great benefit to you. Many of you suffer from time to time with problems related to the ears, sinuses, teeth and throat.

Your sixth house is in Aries, so please also look at the health section on page 49.

CHAPTER 12
Sagittarius Rising

Slav, Teuton, Kelt, I count them all
My friends and brother souls,
With all the peoples, great and small,
That wheel between the poles.
You, Canadian, Indian,
Australasian, African,
All your hearts be in harmony!

Alfred Lord Tennyson

A few words of explanation
A sign on the ascendant expresses itself in a different way from a
Sun sign. However some of the characteristics, even the
childhood experiences, will apply if you have the Sun in
Sagittarius or in the ninth house. They may also be present if

you have Jupiter in Sagittarius or in the first or ninth house. If you have the Moon in Sagittarius or the ninth house, your emotions and reactions will have a Sagittarian flavour. If the ascendant is weak (see Chapter 1), the Sagittarian overlay will not be so noticeable. If the rest of the birthchart is very different from the rising sign, there could be conflict within the personality. This is because the outer manner, the signals which are given out at first meeting by the subject, are very different from the main character which lies underneath. Another possibility is that the subject rejects all that his parents and teachers stood for and creates a life for himself which is very different from the one which they envisaged for him, or the one which he lived through as a child.

Remember that Sagittarius is a mutable, fire sign which implies the ability to adapt to changing circumstances, but also denotes the enthusiasm, energy, intelligence and blind faith which is implied by fire. This is a sign of medium-to-long ascension, which means that there are plenty of you around.

Early experiences
You appear to have been born easily and to have been a wanted child. Your childhood was patchy, with parts of it being good and some parts being diabolical. You learned early in life to switch off and avoid the bad bits. Your parents may have separated from each other but probably not until you had reached a reasonable level of maturity. The problems which you faced could have resulted from situations which were beyond your control, such as a deteriotating relationship between your parents or, on the other hand, conflict between you and your parents. The chances are that, even now, you love them but prefer to live at a distance from them.

You could have found your father too fussy, too disciplinarian or too prejudiced for your free-wheeling taste. There could have been regular rows about the state of your room, your performance at school, or your lack of application to some special interest of theirs ('We spent all that money on violin lessons and now look at you, all you want to do is fish . . .!'). Your parents may have objected to your tendency to disappear whenever some boring chore loomed up on the horizon or conversely, they may have felt relieved when you *did* disappear, because it offered them a welcome respite from your argumentativeness. Your relationship with your father is ambivalent; you may have hated him while you were young but developed respect for him later on. You may have loved and understood him but never learned to communicate with him except by getting into yet another shouting match.

Your relationship with your mother is even worse. You probably saw her as the archetypal mother, the servant of the family who lived her life in a particularly old-fashioned and limited manner. You may have considered her stupid, useless or powerless. The view of your mother as a person who was incapable of making a decision would inevitably reinforce your natural desire for self-determination and independence. Later in life you may have come to understand the difficulties under which she lived and the compromises which she had to make but, even now, you may lack any real respect for her. Whatever the circumstances, you felt cramped, restricted and even immobilized. It is possible that you were disadvantageously compared to a more conventional brother or sister and maybe you felt that you were growing up in a town or an area which had little to offer ('Nothing ever *happens* here . . .!'). Maybe you were expected to follow a strict religious regime in which you had no personal belief, or to conform to a restrictive 'lace-curtain' set of values. Maybe your home life was great, but financial or cultural impoverishment irritated you.

Somewhere along the line you switched off, tuned out and began to look outside the home for some kind of escape route. Many of you worked out while you were quite young that education could offer you a useful way out. You were quick to latch on at school, which earned you the praise of your teachers and the admiration of your peers. You were unlikely to be the victim of bullying, due to your strong wiry frame and your natural aggression. School, therefore, was a natural arena which gave you the precious gift of early success and the opportunity to develop a sense of self-esteem.

As you passed the point of puberty, your family became ever

more exasperated by you. This mattered less and less to you as time went by, because your eyes and thoughts were drawn ever more outwards to the wider world. Your increasingly (to your family's view) unconventional, indeed unacceptable outlook, plus your absolute conviction that there had to be something bigger, better and, above all, newer out there, set the scene for the classic Sagittarian late-teen leap out of the nest.

Here are a few examples of the 'late-teen leap', as supplied by various Sagittarius Sun or ascendant friends and relatives. My aunt left home to get married at the age of 18. Nothing special in this, you might say, but as the younger sister in a 1929 Jewish household, she had to ask her unmarried older sister for her permission first! After marriage, Aunt Anne moved a good distance away from the rest of the family in order to escape from her demanding mother. Mother, accompanied of course by the rest of the household, decided to move as well – taking a house a few doors away from Anne. Poor Aunt Anne! Fortunately for her the marriage was a great success, so all was not lost.

My daughter, Helen, had a good friend called Sharon who, over a period of five years, spent every Sunday and quite a lot of other days at our home. Sharon's father was not a young man, either in years or outlook. He was fussy about the state of the house and from the moment Sharon began to leave childhood behind he and she were at loggerheads. Sharon's mother tried to keep the peace, but nothing helped. The situation was slightly worsened by the fact that Sharon was the middle child and had a conventional older brother and younger sister. After a year or two of secretarial work and a continuation of the pattern of escaping from the house, Sharon took one of those teenage tours of duty on a kibbutz. She left the kibbutz after a few months and in the intervening years has drifted around the world with hardly any possessions, working casually, sleeping on beaches and sending the occasional postcard to Helen. Sharon never includes an address for replies; she is still moving on.

The story of Sharon leads me on to one further point about your youth, or your childhood, and that is of a 'foreign' influence. You may have been the child of immigrant parents, living in one culture whilst at home and another at school. In your teens you may leave not only the parental home, but the parental *country*; learning another language and becoming part of another culture. You probably had a knack for linguistics and an interest in foreign places, but the two-culture situation may be one of your choosing or simply a matter of family circumstances.

Appearance

The chances are that you are slim and raw-boned, with the characteristically Sagittarian lantern jaw. Taken separately, your features are nothing special but when viewed as a whole you are good-looking, often in an unusual way. Even the more chubby and round-faced Sagittarian rising subjects have unusually attractive hair and eyes. Your teeth should be white and even, giving you a wonderful carefree smile. The rounder variety of Sagittarian rising women are often top-heavy, with rounded shoulders and a large bust. Your style of dress is probably outrageous, but whichever style you adopt you stick to it throughout life rather than following fashion.

Outer manner

You are friendly, cheerful and outgoing. You seem to lack the natural caution and fear of new people which other signs display, therefore you appear open and non-hostile even on first meeting. Some of you are in a permanent whirl, chasing around like a demented white rabbit while others affect a superior know-it-all attitude. Some of you have a slow-moving, leisurely manner which belies the quickness of your mind.

You are curious about people and therefore may subject perfect strangers to the third degree. This is usually done quite innocently, you have no intention of hurting anybody. Every new person or situation offers you delightful opportunities to further your knowledge. You try to fit in with any company in which you find yourself whilst actually remaining a distinct individual. You may appear eccentric, even crazy, to strangers, especially over-conventional ones, but the messages you transmit on first acquaintance are usually cheerful and friendly.

You may have a knack for making tactless remarks. This is not done in order to hurt; it simply represents the kind of absolute honesty with which you view the world around you. Some Sagittarians tell me that they 'throw out the wrong image'; this may result from the fact that Sagittarius rising sends out signals of confidence and optimism, which may not be backed up by the nature of the rest of the chart. One Sagittarius rising friend says that she appears tough, but is in reality very soft. Another says he is gregarious at work and in social situations but switches off when at home. Yet another sends out signals which are so confusing that he attracts people whom he really doesn't want to be bothered with. One particularly Sagittarian aspect of your personality is your sense of humour. Whether dry and droll, broad and deliciously vulgar, witty and sophisticated, or innocently childlike, it is your most wonderful attribute. You can be forgiven anything because you brighten up a dreary world and make all kinds of people *laugh*!

Sagittarius characteristics

Whether you were successful at school or not, you continue to learn throughout your life, either by taking courses which help you to progress in your career, or simply because you enjoy intellectual exploration. You could become fascinated by some particular subject such as astrology, or you could have a broad range of interests. Most Sagittarians live very full lives.

As a child you were rarely at home, being busy with the girl guides, cub scouts, sports, animals or anything else that caught your imagination. As you grew up your interests changed, but your level of involvement remained the same. You are happiest when you are fully stretched and totally involved. You simply cannot live without challenge, whether it be intellectual, creative or physical. You can be very creative yourself, but you excel at inspiring other people. Your life can become overfull, and even when you are at home 'relaxing', you are frequently surrounded by relatives, children, animals and noise. You were probably Chinese in a previous life!

You do occasionally feel guilty when you become aware that you are neglecting some aspect of your life (probably your spouse), but this may only cause you to call a *temporary* halt to your frenetic lifestyle. You don't seek an easy life, you need to be successful, and furthermore, to be *seen* as a success by others, but you also want to be loved and to be the centre of every world which you occupy. This is a tall order because one can only take out of any situation, at best, what one puts in. If you neglect your partner, parents, friends etc. sooner or later, they will wander off in search of more rewarding relationships. Some Sagittarians really do prefer to travel lightly, having plenty of friends and acquaintances but very little in the way of permanent relationships or material goods. You may be an eternal back-packer, the zodiac's version of the wandering Jew. This is all very well, but you still need friends and need to feel accepted somewhere. You must guard against using people and then dumping them when they need you. *Be* a friend – don't just *have* friends.

Not all Sagittarians are the outdoor sporty kind; you may be quiet and shy, but your need to stretch yourself and rise to a challenge will still be expressed. You may, for instance, be very fond of gardening, trying new and better ideas out from one year to another, or you may be of a religious or philosophical turn of mind, experimenting with other-worldly ideas for measure. One attribute which is stressed in all astrology books is your high level of intelligence. To be honest, I have never met a stupid Sagittarius rising subject. You really are clever, but you may lack what a friend of mine calls 'follow-through' unless you are in a particularly determined frame of mind. You are full of inspirational ideas. You don't even resent other people taking up your ideas for development, as long as you receive full credit for them. This is in part due to your generosity, but also to the fact that you are a natural teacher, and no one enjoys seeing his ideas being taken up and put to good use as much as a teacher. There is a kind of vicarious satisfaction to be gained from this. You can put up with difficult or unpleasant circumstances for a while but continued frustration makes you cross. Fire signs are not noted for their patience! If you are not allowed to express your anger you can become extremely depressed. Needless to say, your energy, resourcefulness and natural tendency to look out towards the horizon, coupled with your fabulous sense of humour, ensures that you never stay down for long.

Two attributes which you are almost guaranteed to have are

idealism and honesty. You can be devious at times, but rarely crooked, and it would be very hard for you to take advantage of anyone. Your idealism can lead you to keep your head a bit too far up into the clouds. It can be hard for you to come down and get on with the nitty-gritty of daily life. You also have to guard against tactlessness or sheer rudeness in the guise of 'honesty'. Either way, your reluctance to compromise can be your greatest vice or your greatest virtue. You are genuinely broadminded and free from prejudice on grounds of race, religion or colour. You like people who are different because you find them interesting. Your interest in foreigners may lead you to marry someone from a different culture. Even if you don't manage to travel far during your life, you still feel the need to escape, especially if you live in a city. You enjoy the sea, mountains and wide open spaces and if there is nothing better on offer, you enjoy a walk in the country. If you actually live in the country you may choose to work or spend your spare time with animals.

Those of you who are more domestically inclined can be houseproud. However, the usual feeling is that your home is a base, a private retreat and bolt-hole in times of trouble. One aspect of domestic life which you really enjoy is looking after children. You are fond of children and are very loving to your own children, but you cannot spend your life indoors as a housewife (or house-husband), because you need outside stimulation. As a parent you are reasonable, kind and understanding. There is an element of childishness in your own nature which makes you relate very well to youngsters. Youngsters sense that you respect their dignity because you don't talk down to them. Your acting and story-telling ability comes to your aid here as you can both entertain children and effortlessly enter into their special world.

The mid-heaven
This section and those which follow apply only to Sagittarius rising. The mid-heaven shows your aims and ambitions, therefore it can throw some light on your choice of career. In the case of Sagittarius rising births in the UK, and similar northerly latitudes, those of you whose ascendant is in a very early degree

of the sign will have a Virgo mid-heaven while those of you whose ascendant is in the very last degrees of the sign will have a Scorpio mid-heaven. In actual fact, the majority of you have a Libran mid-heaven.

In the USA and southern Europe, about one third of you have Virgo on the mid-heaven while the remainder have Libra on the MC.

Sagittarius/Virgo

This combination produces an adaptable person who is also very idealistic. You have a strong need to serve mankind, either on an individual basis by caring for an elderly or handicapped relative, or on a group basis by working in one of the caring professions. This caring need may also be expressed in a wider way by working for an idealistic movement. Subjects with this MC may choose to work as teachers, social workers, probation officers or in some aspect of the medical profession. Accountancy is another possibility, due to the Virgoan ability to handle figures and the sign's desire to provide a useful service. The travel and transport industries are popular (remember, Virgo is ruled by restless Mercury). You may be drawn to farming, veterinary work, or anything connected with animal welfare. You may be interested in food and nutrition, or you could help people to keep themselves looking good by working in the cosmetics or clothing industries. This combination makes for a very nervy and restless personality but the practicality and seriousness of Virgo coupled with the Sagittarian imagination and optimism could create outstanding success in any profession.

Sagittarius/Libra

By far the bulk of Sagittarius rising subjects come into this category. You are drawn to ambitious projects and large-scale ideas which, if you have the financial resources and a good team behind you, could be extremely successful. Both Sagittarius and Libra are concerned with advocacy. Both signs like to see justice done. Both signs are fascinated by the workings of the law, therefore a legal career is a possibility. You could be equally drawn to spiritual ideas which could lead you into a religious or philosophical way of life. Even if you don't become directly involved in the spiritual world, an element of this will enter your everyday life. The worlds of astrology or psychic matters might appeal to you. Sagittarius rising subjects are highly intuitive and often very psychic. The desire to help man in a more practical way could lead you into politics.

Many teachers have this combination on their charts, as it is naturally Libran to give advice and naturally Sagittarian to teach. Some astrology books associate Sagittarius with further or higher education and the opposite sign of Gemini with primary or secondary schooling, but I have come across Sagittarius rising subjects in all kinds of educational and training jobs. Another traditionally Sagittarian interest is long distance travel, and there are plenty of you working as couriers, travel agents, translators and airline pilots. You get on well with most people and have no prejudice towards foreigners. In fact, you enjoy meeting people from different cultures and looking into different ways of life.

Last but not least, many of you find your way into show business. You are a natural actor and probably a good singer or dancer too, so you could either spend your life actually working in the business or spend a few years on the stage before settling down to a 'proper' job. Many of you retain your interest in stage work and may even return to it later in life. Here are a few real life Sagittarius rising examples. Jennie is a highly qualified computer expert and she also lectures at the University of Sussex. Every Sunday or religious holiday you will find her singing in her local Church choir. Robin is a teacher who spent a couple of years acting before taking his degree and beginning his teaching career. John is an electronics buyer who has a degree in drama. Tony is a bank manager who is deeply involved in amateur dramatics. He tells me that when he retires, he will try to become a full time 'pro'. Mike is a teacher and administrator in adult education; he is very dramatic and very Welsh. It would be amazing if he *hadn't* done his share of singing or acting and Mike has admitted to me that he would have liked to have been an actor. You may be good at, and very interested in competitive sports. Another interest could be the care of animals.

Sagittarius/Scorpio

There are very few people who have this combination. Such a combination stresses the idealistic side of Scorpio which expresses itself in a need to heal. You may, therefore, work in the medical, psychiatric or veterinary fields and you may be a gifted spiritual healer. There is a natural interest in spiritual and psychic matters. The legal interests which are common in Sagittarians might be used directly in forensic work of some kind. You have more patience and determination than the other two MCs, which suggests that you could haul yourself slowly up to a position of great authority and responsibility. You would use your powerful gifts both wisely and firmly.

You are an excellent communicator, therefore you could find work in journalism, radio or television. You like advising and helping the public, so a media career could well be a very good idea for you. A sporting career is also possible, as many of you are excellent sportsmen and women who can make the grade professionally.

Many of us are attracted to people whose Sun sign is the same as our mid-heaven, therefore you could be drawn to Librans, Virgos or Scorpios, depending upon the exact position of your own MC.

The descendant

The opposite point to the ascendant is the descendant which traditionally shows the type of person to whom we are attracted. In the case of a Sagittarian ascendant, the descendant is in Gemini. These two signs have even more in common with each other than do most ascendant/descendant combinations. You are a terrific communicator and a hard worker but, being inclined to take too much on, find relaxation difficult. Being idealistic and highly strung, you need a placid and practical partner to create a balanced relationship. You also desperately need the support of a stable home and family environment. You may have the awkward habit of keeping two relationships on the go at once which could make life just a little bit too crowded for comfort.

You need freedom in any relationship, and are also prepared

to allow your partner to have the opportunity to be a person in his or her own right. You can be cold hearted at times, even to the point of cutting off completely from other people and disappearing inside yourself. As long as you have a measure of friendship in any relationship you can usually make a success of it. At the very least, you are a *relater*; and you are able to keep your lines of communication open. However, most of all, you need to be taken care of, treated like a child on occasion, cuddled and soothed by a very caring partner. You can't live with a possessive or demanding partner and you need to be able to come in and go out whenever you like; you cannot be chained to the house. For some reason, many of you seem to marry Pisceans!

Love, sex and relating – regardless of the descendant

Your need for affection means that you are unlikely to be alone for long; you are a relater and you need company. If your marriage fails you will soon charm someone else into looking after you. Some of you have surprisingly stable marriages. This is probably due to your ability to choose a fairly self-reliant partner, although I suspect that male Sagittarius rising subjects are luckier in this respect than female ones. Females of the species seem to learn how to cope later in life, probably after jumping impulsively into and out of an early marriage.

Sexually, you like to experiment. You are well-known for wanting to see how far you can go, and this may apply to your sexual nature as well. Curiosity could be the main reason for your numerous sexual partners. You could, in the days before Aids, have been a great one-night-stand merchant. Later in life, when some of your curiosity has been satisfied, you settle down more easily to family life. You are one of those people who can actually live quite happily without sex, as long as your creative urges are being satisfied, although you do need attention and affection. You were not cuddled enough as a child and you really do enjoy the sensation of being held and cared for by another. You can also off-set any missing sex by pouring out your energies into sports, hobbies and even the Church. To be honest, sex isn't your problem: your worst enemy is boredom.

As far as friendship is concerned you can be here today and gone tomorrow. Your friendly, open nature ensures that you make friends easily enough, but you tend to drift away and forget them when you move on to other things.

Health

You are either extremely healthy or extremely unfit. To be honest, the chances are that you are rarely ill, but if you do go through a bad patch it can last for quite a few years before you return to full health. You suffer from sporting injuries and silly accidents due to the speed at which you move. Your vulnerable spots are your hips, pelvic area and your thighs, so arthritis, accidents to the legs, and problems related to the femoral artery are possible, while women may suffer from womb troubles. Your nerves can let you down, giving you sleepless nights, skin and stomach problems. If your ascendant is late in Sagittarius, you could have allergies to certain kinds of food and drink.

Your sixth house is in Taurus, so please also look at the health section on page 60.

CHAPTER 13
Capricorn Rising

Nothing to do but work,
Nothing to eat but food,
Nothing to wear but clothes
To keep one from going nude.

Benjamin Franklin King,
The Pessimist

A few words of explanation
A sign on the ascendant expresses itself in a different way from a Sun sign. However, some of the characteristics, even the childhood experiences, will apply if you have the Sun in Capricorn or in the tenth house. There will also be some of these characteristics if you have Saturn in Capricorn or in the

tenth house or even in the first house. If your Moon is in Capricorn or in the tenth house, your emotions and reactions will have a Capricornian flavour. If the ascendant is weak (see Chapter 1), the Capricorn overlay will not be so noticeable. If the rest of the birthchart is very different from the rising sign, there could be conflict within the personality. This is because the outer manner and the signals which are given out on first meeting by the subject are very different from the main character which lies underneath. Another possibility is that the subject rejects all that his parents, parent figures and teachers stood for, and creates a life for himself which is very different from the one which they envisaged for him, or from the one he lived through as a child.

Remember this is an earth sign, which is also cardinal in nature and this implies the desire to make things happen plus the patience and determination to make sure that they do. Capricorn is also feminine/negative in nature which implies introversion and shyness. This is a sign of *short* ascension which means that, as far as births in northern latitudes are concerned, there are not many of you about.

Early experiences

Traditionally, Capricorn rising, or for that matter the presence of the planet Saturn, on the ascendant denotes a difficult birth. One could theorize that because Capricorn is associated with old age, you will have been through a number of previous incarnations, and knowing what is ahead, you don't want to go through it all over again! Whatever the theory, the evidence is that your mother's labour was protracted, painful and dangerous. In the case of one of my Capricorn rising clients, she was born fairly easily – in an ambulance half-way across Ealing Common in the middle of one of the worst bombing raids of the war.

Many Capricorn rising subjects are born to older parents who didn't want, or expect, to have a child at such a late stage of their lives. I can remember a woman called Paula telling me that when her mother was 43 years old she had a very bad attack of indigestion after eating pickled onions. The attack was so severe that her mother paid a visit to her doctor the next day. He told her that she was in the late stages of pregnancy and sure enough, two weeks later, Paula was born. The birth itself wasn't too difficult, but it was worrying, partly due to her mother's age, and also because there was so little time to get anything organized. This birth also took place in London during the war, although the bombing was not too bad due to the fact that a blizzard was blowing at the time! Shortly after this event her father had his first really serious nervous breakdown.

The sign of Capricorn is traditionally assumed to be a sad one indicative of a life filled with limitations and hard lessons to be learned. There is some truth in this idea but the problems are more likely to stem from difficult circumstances than from cruel or unloving parents. This emphasis on hard circumstances is the benchmark of this rising sign. You may have had a difficult relationship with your parents, but this is most likely to be because they themselves were up against hard times. One of your parents, probably your father, may have been a distant figure, either because he was naturally reserved and withdrawn or because his work took up a lot of his time. Your mother might have been strict, but not unreasonable or uncaring towards you. Circumstances dictated that you remain quietly in the background, making very few childish demands and behaving in an adult manner while you were still very young. I always think of this as an old-fashioned sign, because it is associated with the kind of childhood experiences which were far more common in years gone by. This ascendant is probably found more often in third world societies where opportunites for happiness or for creativity in childhood are still unobtainable luxuries.

During your childhood, your parents may have been short of time and money. There may have been too many mouths for them to feed, together with financial setbacks or family illness. You may have had a parent or a sibling who had some form of physical or mental handicap. You could have had an early introduction to the sadder side of life by losing a family member in a particularly tragic manner. This rising sign is the stuff of which all those best selling 'family saga' books are made.

There is another quite different but still typically Capricorn is that your parents themselves had risen from obscurity to become positively wealthy. If, indeed, one or even both of your parents were especially successful or courageous in some way, you may have considered this too hard an act to follow. The effects of this childhood could have led to a number of different reactions on your part, depending upon your basic nature. One possibility is that you did actually follow in their footsteps, while a second is that you gave up the unequal battle and dropped out all together. A third possibility is that you followed a completely different path, finding values which are equally valid but quite different from those of your parents.

Even in the best circumstances, life was difficult for you. You were shy and withdrawn and inclined to hang back and let others step forward and take all the glory (or make bloody fools of themselves). You had little confidence in yourself and may have been afraid of something or someone, either because there was a genuine threat to your safety or as a result of vague fears and phobias. You were finely-built and small for your age, being completely unable to compete with larger, tougher children either on the sports field or in any kind of physical violence. You were a delicate and timid child, a worry to your parents and hard for them to bring up. The fact that you survived at all says a lot about your inner resources of courage and determination; you didn't give up on life then and have been fighting to overcome difficulties ever since.

I would like to add one final thought about your childhood experiences and that is on the subject of *control*. You could well have been dominated or controlled by one or both of your parents; you were certainly taught the value of self-control. This is a very useful technique in most circumstances but it can cause problems when you enter into relationships later on. On the one hand, you may try to control your future partner or on the other, you may find yourself in a relationship with someone who dominates and controls you in the same way that your parents did. Much as you hate the idea of destroying a relationship, you will have to do so if you find yourself a victim of tyranny.

Appearance

Bearing in mind racial differences and variations in birthcharts, the chances are that if you have Capricorn rising you will have rather bony features, with high cheekbones, large eyes and a nice, if slightly toothy smile. These well-defined features could make you extremely good-looking and incredibly photogenic in a 'Garboesque' way or, if the bonyness is extreme, it will make you appear craggy or 'hawk-like'. There is a characteristically Capricorn smile which turns the corners of your mouth downwards rather than upwards, whilst at the same time lighting up your eyes. Your hair is your worst feature, because it is sparse, fine and of a non-descript colour. Men with this rising sign become 'thin on top', while women spend a fortune in the hairdresser on perms and hair colourants, while cursing this ever-present bane of their lives. Your height and physique is small to medium. You could put on a little weight as you get older but, generally speaking, you will remain perhaps just a little below average in height and weight. You choose conservative clothes which might be either city-smart outfits or something cheap and cheerful, according to your lifestyle and your pocket. To be honest, you don't give much attention to your clothing unless you have a special occasion to dress up for.

Outer manner

You are naturally retiring and are the last person to push yourself to the forefront in any kind of new situation. You appear calm, quiet, gentle and modest in social situations, whilst in business situations you are formal and businesslike. The signals you send out to new acquaintances are gentle, kind and practical. You rarely express your feelings publicly, and are a past master at the art of being non-committal. You are not in the least unfriendly; indeed you go out of your way to make others feel comfortable, but you are reserved. Your dry sense of humour is always a delightful discovery to any new acquaintance and your genuinely non-hostile approach to the world ensures that you are surprisingly popular. However, this popularity can vanish under certain circumstances – but more of that later. You are a good conversationalist partly because you usually have something interesting to talk about, but mainly because you are a good and caring listener.

Capricorn characteristics

This section can double up as a brief guide to Capricorn as a Sun sign *or* as a rising sign, so it can provide a handy reference if you want to check up on someone's Sun sign as well as their rising sign.

Yours is a strangely mixed and multi-faceted sign, with many excellent qualities and a couple of really dodgy ones. To add to the confusion there is a kind of accepted set of theories about this sign which don't always stand up when looked at against real people. One such theory is that you are invariably reliable, practical, determined, capable and thorough and, therefore, heading inevitable for a career in banking. Whilst it's true that many of you *are* just like that, other Capricorn rising subjects are ineffectual, undisciplined, prone to vacillation and inclined to leave jobs half-done! This sign, like Scorpio, seems to have suffered from too much astrology and not enough observation! This disparity can, to some extent, be put down to variations in the rest of the birthchart, but it can also be put down to one particularly Capricornian feature and that is your terrible lack of confidence. You may take on a job and then become unsure that you can cope with it or, if something starts to go wrong half-way through, you may simply walk away from it.

This lack of confidence may stem from simple shyness, but in many cases it can be linked to childhood experiences. It is probable that your parents, good as they were, didn't spend much time or energy on you or that they didn't teach you how to value yourself. There is sometimes some kind of educational problem when this sign is rising which means that some of you grow up without learning how to read and write properly. Others of you have a very good basic education but may lack the kind of specialized skills or further education which would allow you to get on in the world. You are proud by nature, refined and rather snobbish and therefore a decent job is necessary for your mental health. A particularly menial job would make you feel humiliated and miserable.

If you reach adulthood without the kind of education and training which will allow you to rise to a position in which you feel comfortable, you will find a way to obtain it in your spare time. Capricorn women escape this kind of difficulty by marrying early, a decision which they may, or may not, regret later on according to circumstances. With or without skills, your ambitious determination begins to show itself quite early and, whether you decide to enter the stock exchange or to become a pop singer, your career direction is steadily upwards towards an unassailable position of respect. You view power and money as being useful but the real motivating force behind your ambition is your need for status, self-respect, self-determination and a decent kind of lifestyle.

Your need for security, coupled with your love of money and status, could lead you to compromise your principles. You could find yourself agreeing to advertise a product which you don't believe in. Alternatively you could cultivate friends for their usefulness, rather than simply for the pleasure of their company.

Capricorns are renowned for being hard workers, and this is very true. Even if some project fails badly, you pick yourself up and, confidence or no confidence, you try again, or you turn your hand to something else. Whatever your chosen field, you are patient, reliable and businesslike and your tenacity makes you particularly successful in any form of self-employment. You have a surprisingly independent outlook and although you make a good employee, you are probably happier in the role of employer. Incidentally, I have discovered that those who earn their living by working alone, as artists, musicians or writers, often have Saturn (the planet which rules Capricorn), close to the ascendant in their birthcharts.

One area in which you excel is family life. Although you enjoy and appreciate friendship, your family comes first and foremost. You are not particularly interested in worldly, ecological or humanitarian issues, unless you have a good deal of Aquarius on your birthchart, but you can be drawn into mainstream politics. In this case, you tend to view your party and those who share your ideology and even your country, as part of your 'family', and therefore your own personal responsibility. It was the

Capricorn President of the USA, Nixon, who extricated America from the Vietnam war, while the very 'tenth-house' character, Adolph Hitler, put German interests so disastrously before those of everyone else. There can be a 'canny' form of nepotism at work here, a kind of personal or political closing of ranks when trouble looms. It is as if the Capricornian need for status and security is, in this situation, extended to cover the wider political 'family' as well as the personal one.

As a parent, you are dutiful, caring and an excellent provider, but you might object to handing out money for frivolities. You could also fall into the trap of exerting far too much control over your offspring. If one of your offspring appears to have any kind of special talent or ability, you will not stint any amount of money or effort to help develop this. You may be a bit on the strict side, insisting on good behaviour, but there is no doubt at all that you truly love your childen. You may moan and grumble when you need to let off steam, but you would be most unlikely to walk away from your responsibilities regardless of any grumbling you may do. Despite all this seriousness, you really do enjoy a good laugh. You have a delightfully dry sense of humour and you genuinely enjoy company and fun.

One subject which is always close to the Capricorn heart is *money*. You can cope with being rich or poor, but you prefer being rich (remember, your eighth house is in sumptuous Leo). You cannot cope under any circumstances with being in debt. Capricorns tend to have a gift for figure work, whether this be balancing the household budget or managing a large organization and you are rarely in the dark about your current personal or business financial position. You are fascinated by money management and are naturally drawn to the world of business, especially the areas of finance and distribution. Unless there are other very outgoing features on your birthchart, you are not really suited to sales work. Even if you work in a field which does not appear at first glance to be particularly businesslike, you still maintain a very sensible and down-to-earth attitude to what you do. Your mind is acute, very shrewd and probably academic but you may have some surprisingly esoteric interests in your spare time. This is the kind of combination which can produce a guy who is an accountant by day and a champion ballroom dancer by night!

You may be very fond of animals, bringing to them the same care and consideration that you do to your family members. Here I will quote my long-suffering father as an example. The care and attention he lavishes on Suzie, my parents' half-feral, androgenous and totally uncontrollable cat, has to be seen to be believed. No matter how many times Suzie comes home hours late, covered with fleas and disporting yet another festering relic of some recent cat-fight on his/her body, Sam's gentle love never wavers. I sometimes think that Suzie is the unacceptable face of Gemini with Aries rising! Fortunately, Sam loves my mother and myself just as fiercely, despite the fact that both of us are as awkward in our ways, if not as sexually peculiar, as is his Suzie.

With your excellent powers of concentration you can work hard and study deeply in order to achieve your ambitions. You find it impossible to understand lazy and feckless people and you don't waste any of your valuable time on them. Your own decisions are taken carefully and sensibly and the time and effort which you invest in any enterprise pays off, even if it takes some time to do so. You might be too materialistic for some tastes and you may be mean in stupid and counter-productive ways. Yours is the sign which squeezes the last drop of toothpaste out of the tube.

You cannot bear to be made to look foolish. When confronted by a person whose sense of humour runs to mockery, you just walk away retaining your dignity. Your own sense of humour is not designed to bring pain to others and indeed you only set out to hurt others on those exceedingly rare occasions when you feel that you have been very badly or unfairly treated. However, even in those circumstances, you prefer to simply walk away from such people and forget that they exist. You may hurt others by concentrating too much on their practical needs, and neglecting their emotional ones, or you may infuriate them by your occasional bouts of petty-mindedness or petty meanness. Your pet fear would be to be placed in an embarrassing or humiliating situation. To be in a hospital, helpless and being dealt with by particularly thoughtless people, would be beyond endurance for you.

You are surprisingly easy to live with and to get along with, never making unreasonable demands upon others. You don't require perfection from other people but you can become annoyed if you feel that they are evading what you consider to be their duty. A Capricorn woman who marries an idle and incompetent guy would try to encourage him to change, and if she didn't succeed, would walk away from the situation. Capricorn, for all its shyness and modesty is, after all a *cardinal* sign, and there is a limit to what you will put up with.

You are not particularly tidy or fussy about your surroundings and you will eat almost anything as long as it is well-cooked and presented. Oddly enough, for such a conservative type of person, you really do enjoy exotic foods. You also enjoy exotic places and will travel the world as soon as you can afford to do so. Visitors are made very welcome, and you usually get on well with your family's friends. It would be most unusual for you to become involved in a silly dispute with neighbours or relatives because you prefer to live in peace with those around you, and discord embarrasses you.

This is, of course, an earth sign which suggests a certain level of sensuality. This might be expressed as a liking for good food, good music and, of course, sexual love as well as much-needed affection. Your hobbies may well express your sensuality too, for example in gardening, cooking, dancing or some gentle and pleasant form of sport.

The mid-heaven
This section and those which follow apply only to Capricorn rising. The mid-heaven shows your aims and ambitions and therefore can throw some light on your choice of career. In the case of Capricorn rising, in northern latitudes such as the UK the majority of you will have your mid-heaven in Scorpio, while those of you whose ascendant is in the last couple of degrees of Capricorn will have Sagittarius on the mid-heaven. In the case of births in the USA and southern areas of Europe, those who have the first few degrees of Capricorn rising will have the mid-heaven in Libra, whilst the rest will have the MC in Scorpio.

Capricorn/Libra

Both these signs are cardinal in nature which suggests that you prefer to make your own personal decisions, although you are co-operative in working partnerships. The Libran MC modifies your Capricorn shyness to an extent which could allow you to be a capable employment or travel agent, personnel officer or financial adviser. You have a natural affinity for figures, which is useful whatever your line of work. The Libran mid-heaven gives you an artistic outlook and a sense of balance, which is useful in situations which require good presentation. You could succeed in the field of marketing, but probably not in straightforward selling as this requires a brashness and confidence which you don't have. You may not excel as a creative innovator, but you are excellent at judging the work of others. You can see at a glance what will work and what will not, and it is this critical faculty which could successfully take you into the world of fashion or publishing.

Capricorn/Scorpio

This is by far the most common combination in the northern hemisphere, and it makes for an uncomfortable mixture of Capricorn caution with Scorpio manipulation. It is possible that you would be drawn to the Scorpionic interests of medicine or police work, where your careful, methodical mind would come in handy. In theory, you would make a brilliant brain surgeon, detective or spy! However, if you decide to eschew these careers in favour of becoming a secretary, greengrocer or childminder instead, you would tackle those jobs with the same energy and diligence. You can be relied upon to do a job thoroughly, so long as nobody rushes or pressurizes you. Your best bet is to tackle one job at a time and do it properly.

The Scorpio MC encourages you to retreat and reflect, which could take you into some kind of research work. You could make a good investigative journalist or scientific author. You have to take care that your outer manner doesn't offend others, especially at an interview, or when trying to get information out of others. You may put on an aggressive or hostile front in order to hide your vulnerability, but remember that others will take you at face value, and thereby miss your finer qualities. The

Scorpio affinity with liquids could take you into the oil industry or shipping.

Capricorn/Sagittarius

This rare combination really doesn't fit comfortably, because the two signs have little in common. However, it is possible that the Capricorn caution, coupled with the Sagittarian optimism and enthusiasm, could combine to make a pretty powerful character. You are drawn to the world of teaching or caring for others in some way. Your practical idealism might lead you into alternative forms of medicine, counselling or even astrology. Your interest in travel and business could lead you to work for an airline or to set up a postal courier service. Alternatively, you could go into some kind of religious occupation or even become a professional mystic or a kind of businesslike Yogi. The sign on the MC can sometimes denote the type of person who we enjoy either working or living alongside. In your case this person might be a Libran, Scorpio or Sagittarian.

The descendant

The opposite point to the ascendant is the descendant. This is traditionally supposed to show the type of person to whom we are attracted. In the case of Capricorn rising, the descendant is in Cancer, which goes a long way towards accounting for the Capricornian love of family life. I have no evidence to suggest that you would go out of your way to choose a Cancerian partner, but I guess that if you did the match would work well because the signs have a great deal in common, both being interested in their homes, families and also in business. However, the emotionalism and moodiness of the Cancerian might irritate you after a while and the combination of these two signs might lead to too much negativity and gloom in the relationship. You'd probably make a better relationship with someone outgoing, who could lift your spirits and also encourage you to stick to your principles.

On the whole, the Cancerian descendant leads you to be very caring towards all those with whom you associate, be they friends, neighbours or working partners. You hate to let anyone down, and therefore are a most reliable person. One black mark which could spoil some of your relationships is your tendency to be mean about small matters. You could be the type who complains about your partner's use of hot water or the way he squeezes the toothpaste tube. However, if your partner is either financially independent, fairly thick-skinned or also rather tight-fisted, none of this will be a problem.

Love, sex and relating – regardless of the descendant

This is where contradictions enter the scene. You are able to live without sex when it is not available, and may indeed choose to do so while you are young. This may be due to shyness or to fastidiousness plus a quite reasonable fear of jumping into bed with someone to whom you haven't been properly introduced! When you are with a regular partner with whom you are comfortable, you can really let your hair down. Remember, this is an earth sign which implies sensuousness. You enjoy the sights, sounds and wonderful feelings that sex in a loving relationship can bring.

You may be flirtatious but your strong sense of propriety, not to mention self-preservation, will probably prevent too much actual tomfoolery on your part. Many of you have a peculiar fail-safe device which comes into operation when you feel threatened by the sexual demands of a partner and that is a tendency towards spinal problems. The equation works like this:

| Capricorn person | + | partner expecting him/her to perform to order | = | slipped disc! |

Health

Apart from the sexually-induced slipped disc, this sign is associated with a range of chronic ailments. You may suffer from rheumatism, especially in your knees. Another typical problem is deafness, possibly associated with some kind of bone problem in the ears or tinnitus. Your difficult childhood may leave you with nervous ailments, such as asthma, eczema and psoriasis, together with chesty ailments such as bronchitis. Despite these annoying problems, Capricorns traditionally live to a ripe old age.

Your sixth house is in Gemini, so please also look at the health section on page 72.

CHAPTER 14

Aquarius Rising

These things shall be! A loftier race
Than e'er the world hath known, shall rise,
With flame of knowledge in their souls
And light of knowledge in their eyes.

John Addington Symonds (English Critic),
New and Old. A Vista

A few words of explanation

A sign on the ascendant expresses itself in a different way from the Sun sign. However, some of the characteristics, even the childhood experiences, will apply if you have the Sun in Aquarius or in the eleventh house. There will also be some of these characteristics if you have Uranus or Saturn in the eleventh house or Uranus in the first house. If your Moon is in Aquarius or the eleventh house, your emotions and reactions will have an Aquarian flavour. If the ascendant is weak (see Chapter 1), the Aquarian overlay will not be so noticeable. If the rest of your birthchart is very different from the rising sign, there could be a conflict in the personality. This is because the outer manner and the signals which are given out on first meeting by the subject are very different from the main character which lies underneath. Another possibility is that the subject rejects all that his parents, parent figures and teachers stood for and creates a life for himself which is very different from the one which they envisaged for him, or from the one which he lived through as a child.

Remember that this is an air sign which is also fixed in nature and the implication is that you are clever and tenacious. If you become attached to an idea, or accustomed to a particular way of life, you will not willingly change. Aquarius is also masculine and positive in nature, which denotes extroversion and courage. This is a sign of short ascension, which means that, in northern latitudes, there are not many of you around.

Early experiences

Aquarius is the least predictable sign of the zodiac, so it is almost impossible to generalize about any aspect of your life. The chances are that you suffered quite deeply sometime during your childhood. There will have been some kind of dramatic or unexpected event which disrupted your life in some way, and this disruption may have had an unexpectedly beneficial side to it. One Aquarius rising subject told me that as a result of war-time evacuation he received a far better education and, indeed, a far better childhood than he would otherwise have had. It is this element of *unpredictability* which is the hallmark of this rising sign. You were the kind of frustrating child who was obviously clever but unwilling to make an effort except at those subjects which excited you. Despite this waste of early opportunities, you caught up later in life and have done very well in your chosen sphere of work. Despite your inability to be cajoled or coerced, you longed for parental approval, especially from your father.

You may have had an excellent relationship with one parent and a prickly, uncomfortable one with the other. Either parent, (but probably the father), could have been extremely moody, resentful, childish, unpredictable and violent. Yours may have been the kind of childhood where your mother tried to protect you from the worst excesses of your father's temper. In a normal childhood, you could still have been subject to periods of unexplained withdrawal of parental affection. If your home situation was actually quite pleasant, you would have been aware of events within the family circle which appeared to be beyond anyone's control. Here are a couple of examples. Edwin's parents had a second child when he was eight years old and this younger brother was born with a severe mental handicap. Stuart, my own son, was terribly upset when his father became severely ill with a heart condition. Happily, the then brand-new operation for a coronary by-pass solved his father's problems. It is interesting to note that the sign of Aquarius is associated with new and experimental ideas and, of course, at that time, by-pass surgery was so new that it *was* experimental.

Your school life could have been disrupted, maybe your family had moved around a good deal which resulted in you attending a variety of schools. Even if this did not occur, the chances are that you didn't do particularly well at school but took up an interest which involved further study later on in life. Some Aquarius rising subjects find it hard to concentrate on anything for long, and if this is your nature you will find that you can grasp new concepts very quickly but then lose interest again just as quickly.

Even as a small child you needed freedom and space and you also needed to be on the move. Like children of the somewhat similar sign of Sagittarius, you were unable to stay indoors for long. You had friends all over the place, and couldn't wait to shoot off out of the house to see them. Yet, despite this need to be out and on the move, you feared the unexpected. It seems that you needed to know that everything was all right at home and in your own private world before you could go exploring. You will have been either very successful or a total failure at school; you were totally incapable of being average. The same situation applied to your outside interests.

There may have been very little pattern to your life. Your

parents might have changed their attitude to you from one day to another, or they may have handed out confusing psychological messages. For example they may have told you that they believed in total honesty, whilst fiddling the tax-man and pinching envelopes from the office. If your parents were reasonable, they may have been thoroughly unconventional. Perhaps one of your parents was particularly successful or gifted. Maybe one of them was a total failure or even a drunken wreck. You yourself were a jumpy, nervy child, being prone to nervous ailments and bouts of peculiar behaviour. If your parents were the caring variety, they would have found you difficult to bring up. If they were the uncaring sort, it is a miracle that you survived at all!

Appearance

Please take into consideration racial differences and the influence of the rest of the birthchart where this is concerned. You are doubtless very good looking. Aquarian women learn to use cosmetics well, because their complexion is pale or sallow. The bone structure of your face is strong, giving you the kind of features which photograph well. Your eyes are probably quite ordinary, plain brown and slightly prominent, but not especially large. However, your highly arched eyebrows draw attention to your eyes, making them look larger than they actually are. Your nose is prominent, (and maybe bent or twisted) and your teeth regular and very white, so your smile is absolutely lovely.

The effect of these well-developed features with your humorous expression, gives you an appearance which is strong and effective. Your hair may be your worst feature, being either a dull brown or turning grey when you are still very young. Female Aquarians overcome this by tinting and perming their hair and nowadays, so do males! You may only be of average height, but you *appear* tall and you don't carry any excess weight. Your choice of clothes is totally individual and possibly even totally outrageous! You may be the very picture of the smartly dressed business person or a complete slob. You may restrict yourself to one colour, for example, never wearing anything but mauve, or you may choose to wear clothes of a bygone age. Most of you prefer casual, rather 'masculine' clothes such as jeans, track-suits and sweaters. You hate frills, patterns and bunches of flowers on your clothing and you are far happier wearing strong plain colours. However, you could easily turn up at a formal function in a frock-coat and Red Indian head-dress! Where clothes are concerned, I wouldn't put anything past you!

Outer manner

Under normal circumstances, you are friendly, open and totally non-hostile. However, if you are faced with someone who is offensive or otherwise unpleasant, you give them absolutely no quarter. You speak your mind and don't fear the consequences. You may be a little shy when you are in an unfamiliar social setting, but once you feel yourself to be at home, you immediately join in with whatever is going on. You are a real asset to a village-green fete! You love meeting new people, and are not at all put off by unusual ones. Your judgement of people is excellent, and you seem to be able to see through surface impressions to the reality which lies underneath. You don't judge people by outer appearances and you cannot be taken in by anyone who puts on airs and graces. Your own approach, apart from being friendly, is businesslike and humorous but not pushy. In some circumstances, you can appear arrogant, or you may give the impression that you class yourself above the people with whom you are associating. When you are with people with whom you are really comfortable, especially if the occasion is a social one, you are terrific. You mix with everyone, thoroughly enjoy yourself and help others to do the same. Your most outstanding quality is your quick wit and sense of humour. Aquarius risers are the masters of the pithy comment and the hilarious one liner.

Aquarius characteristics

This section can double up as a brief guide to Aquarius as a Sun sign *or* a rising sign, so it provides a handy reference for you if you wish to check out a person's Sun sign as well as their rising sign.

Despite your 'super-cool' outer manner, you are quite tense inside. You are a worrier and you hate to feel that any situation is slipping out of your control. You need to be in charge of your own destiny. Like the other fixed signs of Leo, Scorpio and Taurus, you prefer to set your own pace and not to be rushed or hassled by others. When you find yourself placed under severe pressure, you don't crumple up or walk away from the situation but if the pressure is umremitting you become ill. You are capable of running a business of your own, or of having complete charge of a department in a large organization. You can co-operate with others very well, just as long as you are in a position of influence! Where your personal life is concerned, you are a great family member and team worker, just as long as nobody tries to restrict you or dictate to you. Even if you know for certain that you are being stupid, you prefer to be left to make your own mistakes. This doesn't mean that you won't listen to reason; often an opinion given from a person whom you respect is just the thing to help you. However, you are intelligent enough to be able to turn most situations to your own advantage, provided that you don't lose your temper and go at it like a bull at a gate. I know that this next statement is going to come as a surprise to many people, but Aquarians are *moody*!

All fixed signs are moody, because you find it difficult to adapt to changes in circumstances. You can retreat into angry sulking (or become ill) when the world doesn't seem to be going your way. Yours is a very proud sign and you hate to look silly. Perhaps it is just as well that you rarely do act foolishly. You may be surprisingly self-absorbed. You have many friends but you don't enjoy being dragged too deeply into their problems. You have high standards of behaviour but also a high opinion of yourself which can give you an air of arrogance. If someone you respect and care for makes a critical remark obviously you can become upset, but if an outsider criticizes you, it rolls straight off you. Frankly, you are not that interested in the opinions of others. You march to your own drumbeat. You are not easily influenced and will not change the course of your life in order to secure the approval of others. Like all fixed signs, you don't easily abandon either a person or a situation. You cannot be owned or dictated to even by the people whom you most value.

You are a good organizer both at work and at home. Your mind is logical and this is reflected in the way you go about things. There are times when you find it difficult to explain to others why you want things to be done in a particular order or in a particular way, so you may need to pay a little more attention to developing good communication skills. You need to find a career that you enjoy. There must be an element of play involved with your work or you will become bored which will lead you to switch-off completely. You need to be in an environment where you can meet and influence new people. You must have the opportunity to exercise your mind and to use your capacity for lateral thinking. Under normal circumstances you are quite lazy, but when you decide to go after something, or someone, no one is more determined.

Yours is an unusual household. You prefer a clean, tidy and well-appointed home with elegant furniture and fittings and, therefore, you spend a good deal of your time and money on your home. You are a good cook and a good host, making guests feel really comfortable and welcome. The unusual aspect comes from your personal interests. There is a very good chance that you own at least one computer and a variety of other electrical gadgets, especially radio and recording equipment as well as good kitchen equipment. Your bookshelves reflect your esoteric tastes. You accumulate books and you may have a large collection. Your home may be overflowing with magazines, videos, papers, brochures and filing cabinets. There might be a great quantity of equipment stuffed into your garage and kept there 'in case'. This collection of books and other gear reflects the comings and goings, over the years, of your many hobbies and interests.

You enjoy being part of a family and you are an excellent parent. You will probably continue to study in adulthood, and you encourage your partner to do so as well. You will provide your children with as much education as they can stand and will encourage them to take up all kinds of spare-time interests and hobbies. Your rational attitude may be a bit of a drawback in relationships, because you may not find it easy to understand the emotional needs of others. When your partner is looking for sympathy and understanding you may come to respond a little *too* reasonably and logically. You must learn to see the emotional needs, both of yourself and of others. In addition to being logical, you are also intuitive and even, perhaps, psychic. This side of your nature might also take some coming to terms with. Where other family relationships, such as those where parents and in-laws are concerned, you like to maintain good lines of communication with them but not to be over-involved in their lives.

Traditionally, Aquarians are supposed to belong to all kinds of groups and organizations but this is far less so in the case of Aquarius rising. Your independent nature makes you very friendly but not necessarily a good group or committee worker. You may wish to campaign for a particular charity or to make a political point, but once you have achieved your aims, you disengage yourself and sink gratefully back into privacy. Perhaps Aquarius rising subjects dislike having too many obligations and attachments taking up their precious store of spare time. You will help someone on a personal basis, as long as they show some willingness to help themselves; you are impatient with whiners and emotional drainers. You are also not particularly good with sick people, and you may lose patience with them once the immediate crisis is over. You cannot under any circumstances have respect for shirkers, moaners or perpetual 'victims'.

The friendliness of an Aquarian rising subject differs a little from that of the Sun in Aquarius. Both of you are remarkably unprejudiced and have no dislike of people on grounds of race, colour, social class or religion and both like meeting new people, but the Aquarius rising subject lacks patience and may drift away if the friend becomes too demanding. Another slight difference is that the Aquarius rising subject definitely prefers youth to age and will choose his friends from the younger set, whereas the Sun Aquarian isn't so particular.

You are honest and reliable, therefore you keep your promises and hate to let anyone down. You find it hard to understand those who don't share your high standards. You dislike walking away from commitments, but you can be unrealistic in your aspirations. One example might be a woman who takes on a business which lacks any real viability. Another example might be of a guy who goes on loving a girl who doesn't really want him. This inability to separate reality from dreams is typical of an air sign and it can cause you some really awful problems. Your reliability and kindheartedness makes you a truly wonderful friend, but if someone turns against you or begins to laugh at you, you become exceedingly sarcastic and hurtful in self-defence. One final, rather daft point which I would like to make is that all the Aquarian rising subjects whom I have met are extremely faddy about food. Some are vegetarians while others are very plain eaters, while there are others who are totally impossible to cater for.

The mid-heaven

This section and the ones which follow apply only to Aquarius as a rising sign, and not as a Sun sign. The mid-heaven is traditionally supposed to indicate the subject's aims and ambitions and, therefore, can show the type of career to which one is attracted. When Aquarius is on the ascendant, Sagittarius is *always* on the MC. These two signs are very similar, therefore the kind of personality which is projected by the ascendant has a similarity to the subject's ultimate aims in life. To put this into plain English, unless there are a good many planets (including the Sun) hidden in some crafty sign such as Scorpio or Cancer, what you see is, more or less, what you get!

You need freedom and you cannot stand being restricted, dictated to or bullied. You could succeed as a journalist, delivery-driver, racing-driver, travel courier or sales representative; in short, anything which gives you an opportunity to get out and about and meet new people. You look at the world with fresh eyes and bring new concepts to everything you touch, so you are very useful in solving technical problems. Your obsessive nature can be useful here because, when you want to, you can toss aside your languor and work away at a problem until it is solved. Although you can succeed in any technical field, the most obvious ones include electronics, telecommunications and computers. You are intelligent and quick on the uptake and you have a good memory, therefore it would be stupid for you to take a job which didn't stretch your mind.

Your interest in scientific research could take you into the fields of physics, medicine or even horticulture, but your balanced mind and natural arbitration skills could lead you into law. You are a skilled negotiator which could suggest either straightforward legal work or something similar, such as Trades Union negotiations. Another typically Sagittarian career which might interest you is teaching. There is an element of the actor in you which, coupled with your desire to help others, makes you a natural teacher or training officer. The independence of this kind of job would appeal to you as well. There is one more career which might attract you, and that is the world of show business. Many of you are natural actors, singers, dancers or musicians. Your unusual mind could make you a successful inventor or a wonderfully creative and imaginative writer, especially if the rest of your birthchart leans that way too.

Aquarians like to look laid-back and easy-going but this is a pose. You are ambitious and money-minded. You enjoy status. This means that you need a good position within your job and a career which in itself is admired or envied. An eminently suitable position might be the director of an independent radio station! You also like money. You don't need to accumulate money in order to feel secure or to gain power over others, but simply in order to have a comfortable, even luxurious, standard of living.

There is a side to your character which I have left until now, and this is your attraction to mysticism. In your case, this goes beyond the realms of a hobby or vague interest and becomes an integral part of your life's direction. You may become directly involved with a religious organization, either in an established Church or Temple, or you may be attracted to something less orthodox. The Aquarian side will encourage you to take a scientific look at such subjects as astrology, graphology and numerology, while the Sagittarian side will urge you to seek spiritual development. Therefore, you could become minister of the Church, a medium or healer, an astrological counsellor, a holistic or alternative health therapist, or a yoga teacher. There is such a strong pull towards the scientific side of spiritual or metaphysical investigation, which makes it inevitable that you will look for and follow some kind of spiritual path. Whether this remains a part of your private life or whether you decide to make a career of it depends partly upon personal preference, and partly upon the amount of influence your spiritual guides decide to exert upon your life. It is certain that you will go through a number of problems and crises in your life, and it may be at such a time that you begin to feel the need to explore the world of metaphysics and philosophy.

The descendant

The descendant, or cusp of the seventh house, is traditionally supposed to throw light on our attitudes to partnerships and may even indicate the type of person whom we choose to marry. In the case of Aquarius rising, the descendant is in Leo.

There is no evidence that you are especially attracted to Leos, but you do find them easy to understand because you have a good deal in common with them. Your personal standards are high, you are proud, dignified, obstinate and tenacious. It is possible that you could work well together, but I doubt whether two such egocentric people could actually manage to live together for very long. In general, you seek a partner who is intelligent, independent and good-looking! Your partner must have something to offer which is just that little better than the average. You might be attracted to a show-business personality, a high-status business-person or a scientist of high repute. All this will work out very well just as long as your partner can offer you the kind of love, affection, attention and emotional security which you need. You cannot be fettered or smothered and you don't seek to smother your partner but you cannot be ignored and, when your confidence takes a knock, you need to be cuddled, loved and understood. It is possible that your requirements from a relationship are a little unrealistic, and you suffer a certain amount of disappointment. When you learn to adjust your sights a bit lower, your relationships improve. If you are female you will need a career of your own; you can't bear to sit indoors waiting for hubby to come home and slip you a bit of pocket money.

Love, sex and relating – regardless of the descendant

Despite your need for reassurance, you find it hard to give this to others. Your detached attitude and your tendency to give logical answers to emotional questions can leave your partner feeling misunderstood. Your need to travel on an inward, spiritual journey must be understood, and it is best if your partner has the same kind of spiritual interests. If you were to marry an extremely practical and earthy type neither of you would understand each other for one minute. Oddly enough, you have to guard against too much tenacity in relationships because you can hang on far too long to someone who no longer needs you or even abuses you.

You are very active sexually and you are an inventive and exciting lover. However, the most important ingredients in a relationship must be intelligence, humour, shared interests and *friendship*. If the sexual side is good as well, then hooray! You may go through an experimental stage where you separate love from sex, having a variety of partners, some for loving friendship and others for sex. Once you are settled into a permanent relationship, however, you are the faithful type, as long as your partner treats you decently. You are completely turned off by a lack of personal hygiene. I can remember one Aquarius rising subject commenting drily to me that he 'gave the girl up because you could fry fish in the grease on her bra straps'. Finally, you don't fall in love easily but when you do so, you fall very very hard. It's that romantic child-like Leo descendant which catches you out.

Health

The traditional weak points for this sign are the ankles; so you must guard against phlebitis, thrombosis and accidents to the feet and ankles. Apart from this, I have discovered that Aquarius rising subjects have a great deal of trouble with their ears, noses and throats. You may suffer from hay-fever, asthma, allergies which give you runny eyes and thyroid trouble. Your teeth are either very good, or very bad. You do have a nice smile, so if your teeth begin to present problems it would be wise to cultivate a good dentist. You could also be subject to back problems, especially when you are going through a period of stress and tension.

Your sixth house is in Cancer, so please also look at the health section on page 84.

CHAPTER 15
Pisces Rising

We are the music-makers,
And we are the dreamers of dreams,
Wandering by lone sea-breakers,
And sitting by desolate streams;
World-losers and world-forsakers,
On whom the pale moon gleams:
Yet we are the movers and shakers
Of the world for ever, it seems.

Arthur O'Shaughnessy, *Ode*

A few words of explanation
A sign on the ascendant expresses itself in a different way from a
Sun sign. However, some of the characteristics, even the
childhood experiences, will apply if you have the Sun in Pisces

or in the twelfth house. There will also be some of these characteristics if you have Neptune in Pisces, or the first or the twelfth house. If you have the Moon in Pisces, your emotions and reactions will have a Piscean flavour. If the ascendant is weak (see Chapter 1), the Piscean overlay will not be so noticeable. If the rest of the birthchart is very different from the rising sign, there could be a conflict within the personality. This is because the outer manner and the signals which are given out on first meeting by the subject are very different from the main character which lies underneath. Another possibility is that the subject rejects all that his parents, parent figures and teachers stood for, and creates a life for himself which is very different from the one which they envisaged for him or the one which he lived through as a child.

Remember that this is a water sign which is also mutable in nature suggesting emotionalism and changeability. Pisces is also feminine/negative which implies introversion, shyness and a caring nature. This is a sign of very short ascension which means that, in northern latitudes at any rate, there are very few of you around. Oddly enough, even in southern latitudes this sign does not have a particularly long period of ascension, therefore, on our planet at any rate, you are a truly rare fish.

Early experiences
If you have the misfortune to be born with Pisces rising, you could have experienced a truly horrific childhood. As I explained in the previous section, there are technical reasons for there being so few of you around, but there could be a few non-technical ones too. You grew up in a 'mother-dominated' household. Your father may have been severely incapacitated by illness or simply a very weak and ineffectual character. He may have died while you were young, or he may have deserted the family, leaving your mother to cope alone. Your mother was probably strong enough to cope with this, but she may have become embittered or self-pitying as a result.

Some Pisces children have very poor health. The heart, lungs and bronchial tubes are weak, and there may be other problems as well. I have no real evidence of this, but my instinct and intuition tells me that many potential Pisces rising lives may be lost through birth defects, infant mortality and accidents. I suspect that a good many of those children who spend their lives in hospitals or institutions have this ascendant. I am even prepared to bet that a number of children who die from neglect or abuse have this rising sign. The best that one can say about it is that if you survive into adulthood, there will come a time when the ascendant progresses from Pisces into Aries, bringing a change in your luck as well as a change in your attitude to life.

Your problems began while you were still inside your mother's womb! At that point in her life your mother may have been unhappy, unhealthy or short of money and in no shape to have a baby! Your entry into the world was difficult and dangerous, and your survival over those first few weeks was in doubt. Even as a small child you had the look of an 'old soul'. You seem to have entered this world with the remnants of a previous life still clinging to you, although of course, nobody had the time to notice this. It seems that you are born to fulfil some kind of karmic debt, at least during your early years! The suffering which you underwent as a child could have arisen in a number of ways. If you were the type of Pisces rising child whose health wasn't good, there would have been occasions when you were so ill that you were not expected to recover. You may have spent some time away in hospital, or in a school for delicate children. Even if you were not sent away, you would have spent a good deal of time alone in bed, reading and thinking. It is this enforced withdrawal from life which allowed your creativity and your imagination to develop. The following examples will help you understand the problems.

Eve was the fifth child, born prematurely to parents who needed a fifth child like they needed a hole in the head! In fact, they went on to have a sixth child who, incidentally has the Moon in Pisces, whom they needed even less! Eve was evacuated during the war and this did not prove to be a happy experience for her. She spent her time away from home feeling lonely and desolate. Soon after returning home, she contracted rheumatic fever and was sent away once again, to a special school for delicate children. It was while Eve was at this school that she discovered that she had a talent for sport. She made some friends and really began, for the first time, to enjoy life. Soon after her return to the family, her father left home for good. Eve has told me that she never went short of the basic necessities of life, but there were no luxuries, and little love.

Margaret was adopted under peculiar circumstances (money changed hands). Her adoptive parents were neither young enough nor sufficiently competent to handle the reality of bringing up a boisterous child. Her mother had dreamed of raising a piano-playing, beribboned dolly, whilst Margaret was a gangling, overgrown, uncontrollable hoyden. Her adoptive father was a quiet, withdrawn little man who, in his non-communicative way, actually loved Margaret. Her adoptive mother was the type of woman whose upwardly mobile urges were forever doomed to be frustrated. Mother soon grew to dislike Margaret, and sought various ways of getting her out of the house. Margaret spent a good deal of time with a variety of 'aunties', who were cajoled and bribed into looking after her, until around the age of seven or eight, she developed a 'shadow on the lung' and was sent away to a school for delicate children. It was while she was at this school that Margaret discovered a talent for art and sport. The school strongly favoured the outdoor life and introduced Margaret to horticulture, which developed into a life-long passion. Eventually, Margaret came home. She grew even closer to her father. Her somewhat masculine nature made her a good companion to him, and she learned to share his interests of gardening, do-it-yourself and fixing up the car. However, just as this rapport was firmly established, it was suddenly destroyed due to the fact that her father had a stroke which left him partially paralysed and unable to speak. Both Eve and Margaret 'escaped' into marriage while they were still in their teens, and both went on to have a number of children.

Your health may have been all right, but you would still have been lonely and unhappy a good deal of the time. A Pisces rising girl called Michelle, told me that her father left her mother to bring up two children (Michelle and her younger sister) on her own. Her mother had to work, of course, but also enjoyed a great social life with many boyfriends, holidays and outings, leaving Michelle in charge both of the household and her younger sister from a very early age. Despite this, Michelle did well at school, learned to speak a number of languages, and became a courier in the travel trade.

It is just possible that your home life was quite reasonable, but that you were not on the same wavelength as the rest of the family. You may have preferred to laze about in your room, playing music and drawing, rather than helping with the chores or getting on with your studies. If you were this type of Piscean you would eventually have drifted away from the family and made a life for yourself among like-minded people elsewhere.

In your own case, your education may have been good, bad or indifferent. You seem to have had plenty of opportunity to develop your talent for sports, art and dancing, even if the rest of your education was poor. It is possible that you found it difficult to relate either to your teachers or to some of the other children. The children, or worse still, the teachers, might have taken it upon themselves to bully and torment you. Whether this was the case or not, you may have 'switched-off' during childhood, returning to the world of education in adulthood, either through evening classes or by teaching yourself. One can guarantee that you will become an authority on some subject of your own choice later on. With Margaret, it is gardening and the language and culture of Middle-Eastern nations; with Eve it is the psychic and spiritual side of life. Other Pisceans whom I have met are mathematicians, historians, artists, language specialists, or skilled sports and dance teachers.

Appearance

Bearing in mind racial factors and the rest of the birthchart, you should be of medium height and size, with a pale, translucent complexion and fine blonde hair. I have seen Piscean eyes described in an astrology book as, 'being like a semitic blowfish'. There is some truth in this. Your eyes are probably very pale grey or grey-blue in colour and they may be large and lustrous, or simply prominent. Women of this sign spend a good deal of time and money perming and lightening their pale, flimsy hair. Nowadays, male Pisceans also perm and colour their difficult hair. You are slim when young but inclined to put on weight later in life, especially if you give up smoking. One of your best features cannot actually be seen, and that is your voice. You have a quiet, gentle and humorous voice which is pleasant and relaxing to listen to. Your choice of clothes is casual and sporty, but not especially unusual. You prefer to put something on and then forget it rather than to try to create an 'image' and you are not especially self-conscious about your appearance. Oddly enough, you may be fussy about the colour of your clothes, preferring to stick to one or two colours which you feel comfortable with.

Outer manner

Under normal circumstances you are friendly, non-hostile and welcoming to new acquaintances. You project a gentle, helpful, kindly openness, and your ready wit and considerable intelligence makes you fun to be with and a very pleasant friend. The problem is that you are not totally reliable, because you prefer to drift in and out of people's lives rather than becoming a permanent fixture. You can be incredibly hostile to anyone who looks as if they might take it upon themselves to talk down to you. In business situations you appear intelligent, sensible, capable and very quick to pick up the essence of the situation. However, you are an excellent actor and, therefore, you can fit into any kind of company or situation. One aspect of your personality which you find hard to hide is your irritation when under pressure. You can become tense, tetchy and surprisingly nasty. Maybe this is the real you!

Pisces characteristics

This section can double up as a brief guide to Pisces as a Sun sign *or* as a rising sign, so it provides a handy reference for you if you wish to check out someone's Sun sign, as well as their rising sign. You may find that other factors on your chart swamp the Piscean influence so that the usual astrological tendency for the ascendant to be on show, while the other features on the chart are hidden, may be reversed. However, for the time being, we will concentrate on the Pisces element in your birthchart.

The sign of Pisces, as we all know, is represented by the

image of two fish which are swimming in different directions. I
have noticed that there are two distinct types of Piscean, one
which represents the practical fish, while the other represents
the nebulous, chaotic, dreamy one. Most of you appear to lean
towards one of these two natures, whilst having at least a touch
of the other one about you somewhere. If you are one of the
practical types of Piscean, you will be very attached to your home
and family. You have a great longing for a nice home of your
own and, if you are lucky enough to eventually obtain one, you
will spend a good deal of time and money keeping it in apple-pie
order. You may collect antiques, keep a wonderful garden or
become the do-it-yourselfer of the century.

Both sexes will be excellent cooks, but you have to watch that
your own love of food doesn't spoil your figure. You are
surprisingly ambitious, needing to reach a position of status and
respectability. This may be a reaction to what you saw as your
parents' dereliction of their duty. If your childhood was
reasonably normal, then your parents may have made you feel
inadequate in some way which, in turn, also leads you to become
ambitious. Whatever the childhood situation might have been,
the reaction is the same. You want to get on in life! This may be
surprising news to those of you who are used to reading
astrology books which stress the dreamy, non-materialistic side
of the Piscean nature. If you don't have any great ambitions for
yourself, you certainly will have them for your children. In the
meantime, you need a comfortable, attractive and secure home
and will go to great lengths to see that you get this.

Now we will take a glimpse at the other Piscean fish. It is
worth remembering that Pisces is a *mutable* sign which denotes
restlessness and changeability. You are a dreamer and a
fantasizer, and your dreams may take you in any number of
different directions. This intuitive and imaginative side of your
nature is probably inborn, but your unhappy childhood
definitely helped to foster it even more. You spent a good deal of
time imagining what life would be like, thinking if only . . . 'I
were a princess; I won a million pounds; I became the world
champion snooker player . . .' You may have spent a good deal of
time alone, either by choice or by force of circumstances, and

this too allowed you to stretch your imagination by reading, dreaming, thinking and generally fiddling around. You may be so emotional that you don't know what you are going to say (or feel) next.

This lonely, introspective childhood will have given you the time and space to develop your creative and intuitive abilities. You may have become an excellent artist or musician, you may make up marvellous children's stories, or you may be able to inspire others in order to make their dreams come true. You could be drawn to the world of metaphysics; perhaps in the form of astrology, mediumship, white (or not so white) witchcraft, or some kind of old religion, such as Druidism. You will be driven to search for a deeper meaning to life and the hereafter. Whether you take the route of deep religious and philosophical thought, or simply a fascination with ghost stories, it is merely a different manifestation of the same urge. You need to escape from our everyday world of practical matters and endless chores in order to delve into the far distant land of beyond. If I do a quick mental round-up of my Sun in Pisces or Pisces rising friends and relatives, I come up with devout Jews, spiritual mediums, spiritual healers, dowsers and ley-line hunters, astrologers and Tarot readers, palmists, regression hypnother-apists, artists, writers and musicians. All of them are canny, sensible, capable and hard-working, but all are equally involved in the search beyond our everyday world for the world which lies hidden beyond the veil.

Now let us take a look at both of the fish on one plate, so to speak! You have a great desire to help others and even to sacrifice your own needs for the sake of others but I'm not sure that your motives for this are altogether altruistic. You may have a need to see yourself as the soul of goodness; you may wish to see yourself as the knight in shining armour. If you insist on continuing to live in unhappy or awkward circumstances, you should look inside yourself and examine your motives in order to see what it is that you are gaining from the situation before bemoaning your fate to everyone around you. Nevertheless, you are absolutely wonderful in a crisis. If anyone, even a new acquaintance, turns to you for help, you immediately understand the problem and act at once to solve it. You can be a great worrier. You may worry about your health, your family or the imminence of a nuclear holocaust and, if you have nothing to worry about, you will go and look for something. You care about small matters and rarely stop to think whether the situation which is currently on your mind is really worth all the anguish. Any form of injustice upsets you and brings you immediately to the defence of the underdog. If it happens that an animal is being ill-treated you really lose your temper and go all out to rescue the poor creature. As it happens, some Pisceans relate better to animals than to people, while most love to own animals and look after them. You have no prejudices against people on the grounds of race, religion or colour. Indeed, you like your friends to come from diverse backgrounds because this makes them all the more interesting.

Where practical matters are concerned you can be surprisingly careful. For example, you hate unnecessary waste and will re-use old envelopes and save paper bags and so forth, for a rainy day, You may never be rich, but you hate to be in debt, and you usually have a few pounds tucked away somewhere for emergencies. You don't like to borrow money, or to be under any kind of obligation to others, but you quite like it when others are under an obligation to you as this fulfils your need for self-sacrifice while, at the same time, giving you a small measure of control over them. One thing you do hate, however, is to be owed money. If at all possible, you will chase up a debtor; if the debt is not repaid you will never forget and never trust the defaulter again. Your strong sense of self-preservation saves you time and again from disaster, and you can be very canny when it comes to making sure that your needs are met.

You never forget a hurt, but equally so, you never forget the person who has helped you either. Being a consummate actor you won't necessarily appear to react when you are hurt, but you won't forget either. Your sensitivity and vulnerability are such that you never learn to develop a thick skin. You are just as easily wounded by a nasty remark or by cruelty or treachery in adulthood as you were when you were a child. Your sensitivity to atmosphere is phenomenal, and it is this which makes it possible for you to capture feelings so easily in paint, words or music. Some of you take this sensitivity and awareness and develop it into clairvoyance, mediumship and the ability to 'feel' the future.

Pisceans are relaters. You are probably married (often more than once), or living with someone. You very likely have children around you, and you are in fairly frequent contact with your parents. You also have contact with ex-spouses, ex-in-laws and Uncle Tom Cobbley and all! You are not short of relatives and you get on with all of them amazingly well, just as long as they don't try to remake you or to bully you. Friends are important to you but, much as you like people, you also need time and space for yourself. You need freedom – even if you live the most well-regulated of lives you don't appreciate being asked how long you are going to be away and what time you will be back. You can be both strong and weak, selfish and giving, malleable and obdurate, meek and bossy, reliable and untrustworthy – in fact, a total conundrum. You resent criticism because you rarely see yourself clearly and don't want to be faced with the truth.

Some Pisceans are abstemious, non-smoking, frugal eaters, who never touch as much as an aspirin, while others are deeply into all forms of self-indulgence and self-destruction. Some of you are dreadful hypochondriacs, while others are amazingly forbearing under the weight of truly dreadful ailments. It is a rare Piscean who is truly happy, wealthy or healthy!

One aspect of your personality which is typical of the sign is your moodiness. Another is the duality of your nature; the two fish again, I suppose. Firstly, let us examine the moods. What you wanted passionately on Monday, Tuesday and Wednesday may not suit you at all on Thursday. You may even change moods each six hours, as the tide turns! The duality of your nature ensures that you can be all sweetness and light on one occasion, and amazingly spiteful on another. You are willing to help others with all your might but when they finally land on their feet you can be consumed with jealousy at their success. You are rarely happy because too much contentment bores you, yet you can be extremely cheerful when living under the most difficult of circumstances. You love a crisis, but cannot take too much strain. You are a mass of contradictions, and you react to everything on an emotional level; no one, least of all yourself, can understand you.

The mid-heaven
The mid-heaven is supposed to show the subject's aims and ambitions, therefore it can throw light on his choice of career. In the case of Pisces rising, the MC is always in Sagittarius.

You could be attracted to the Sagittarian careers of teaching and training, or the Piscean ones of social and medical work. Both signs have a strong urge to help people and to relieve suffering, therefore you may be drawn to work in some institution, such as a prison, a hospital, a mental hospital or a home for old or disabled people. Your desire to help and care could take you into child care or nursery nursing, while the Piscean attachment to feet could lead to a career in chiropody. Many Piscean subjects make a career out of caring for animals. You are deeply interested in art and music, and may take these up as a career. If you cannot follow a creative career, you will continue to develop your creativity in the form of a hobby. Hobbies and part-time jobs, such as dressmaking and gardening might help to fill this gap, as would self-expression in the form of pottery, metal-work or even singing. You may fulfil your need to care for others by some form of voluntary work, possibly attached to a hospital. Your strong sense of justice could lead you into a legal career, or into one which requires a talent for arbitration and administration.

Both Pisces and Sagittarius are deeply interested in religion and philosophy, so this will figure strongly in your life. You may become involved in some kind of organized religion or take an interest in spiritual and mediumistic work and spiritual healing. You could take up this kind of work on either a full or a part-time basis. Another interest which both these signs have in common is travel. Pisceans are restless and are often drawn to water, so a career on the sea is possible. Fishing is another Piscean interest, so you could take this up as either a job or a hobby. Your talent for languages, combined with your itchy feet, could take you travelling around the world, either in connection with your work or as a hobby. Your restless nature is best suited to a job which takes you around the country rather than one which involves sitting still in one place. You may work from home on some kind of private project, travelling out for purposes of research or observation. Writers and artists of one kind or another would fall into this category. You may teach others from your own home, holding 'workshop' sessions on your own specialized subjects. You need variety in your work and you also need to meet a variety of people. Many of you are not actually suited to work at all, and may be better off with a private income or to being kept by someone else. I have noticed that Piscean subjects have a peculiar kind of love/hate relationship with motor cars. You either love them and are an excellent driver, or you hate to drive and rarely do so. A great many of you never get around to learning this skill and, for all I know, never feel as if you are missing anything. Water is another Piscean oddity, you either love it so much that you include it into your work or your hobbies; or you hate it.

The mid-heaven can sometimes show the type of person with whom we are comfortable, either in working partnerships or even as marriage partners. In the case of Pisces rising, this would suggest a strong affinity with Sagittarians.

The descendant

The descendant, or the cusp of the seventh house, is traditionally supposed to show the type of person to whom we are most attracted. In the case of Pisces rising, the descendant is in Virgo. This does not mean that Pisceans make a point of marrying Virgoans, but it does suggest that your first experience of marriage will have a Virgoan flavour to it. This situation would involve you in much sacrifice and hard work, in return for very little in the way of respect or affection. After such an inauspicious start, you will probably move on and find another partner who is, at least, a little more affectionate.

The Virgoan influence is also expressed in the way you conduct your marriages. You look after your partner very well, and you will put up with a good deal of restriction or even unpleasantness, if necessary. You cope with this by switching-off and letting your mind roam elsewhere away from the reality of your day-to-day life. If you are lucky, you will be able to find someone who represents the better Virgoan values, and who is reliable, competent, hard-working and decent. You may marry initially for security, or in order to escape from your parents. You may even marry for sex! However, if you do make a mistake the first time around, you will look later for someone who shares your interests, is willing to communicate with you and also offer you a peaceful, decent homelife.

Love, sex and relating – regardless of the descendant

Pisces is a very sexy sign! However, you may live for years with a poor lover. You need to give and receive love and affection, possibly because you were deprived of it when you were a child. You are able to divert your sex-drive into some kind of 'higher purpose', such as religion or good works of some kind. Being long-suffering and self-sacrificing, you may continue to live for years with a partner who doesn't please you sexually, or you may learn to live entirely without sex by diverting your love into the care of your children. Given a chance to express your sexuality you can really make the sparks fly. Your vivid imagination and your taste for fantasy may lead you into some very peculiar situations. You are generous and fond enough of play to indulge your partner's need for fantasy, so really, with you, anything goes.

Your partner must take account of your moods, however, because the very thing which you most wanted for the last few months may totally turn you off on the next occasion. Your sensuousness and delicate sense of touch, together with your delight in relaxing and throwing yourself into a whirlpool of sensation, gives you the ability to enjoy the full pleasure of sex in all its forms. If you are the 'water baby' type of Piscean, you will love to make love in the bath!

Health

Traditionally, you are supposed to have bad feet and it is often the case that your feet do give you problems. They are very sensitive, and are apt to swell up when you are overtired or overworked. Other than your feet, almost anything and everything can go wrong with your health. Your lungs and heart may be weak, as may be your spine. Females tend to suffer from menstrual problems, while both sexes will have difficulty in balancing their body fluids. This may result in high blood-pressure, cystitis, varicose veins and a host of other problems. However, despite your poor health, you usually manage to live a full and long life.

Your sixth house is in Leo, so please look at the health section on page 94.

PART THREE

Deeper and Deeper

If you have an analytical mind and enjoy looking beyond the obvious, you might enjoy exploring some of the ideas which I have set out for you in the following sections. I have taken a look at such features as 'cuspy' ascendants, the decanates of each sign and the influence of the immum coeli plus the effect of planets which are in conjunction with the ascendant.

CHAPTER 16
The Immum Coeli

The immum-coeli (or nadir), usually referred to as the IC, is at the bottom of the birthchart, directly opposite to the mid-heaven. This refers to the private side of one's life, the home and the family. Traditionally, the IC also refers to the beginning and ending of one's life, the mother or mother-figure, and any kind of ancestral memory. Here is a very brief outline which shows the effects which each of the 12 signs of the zodiac might have when on the IC.

Aries
There may have been some kind of conflict going on in the family at the time you were born. However, your childhood environment was cheerful and your parents helpful and encouraging. Your adult home is an open and friendly place with many visitors and a lot of fun and noise. You could fill your home with gadgets or sports equipment.

Taurus
Your birth should have been comfortable and well arranged and, if your early environment was lacking in either material or emotional comforts, you can rest assured that your later life will make up for this. Your own adult home will be full of music and beauty and probably over-furnished and full of souvenirs.

Gemini
This sign suggests a strange start in life, possibly due to some kind of disruption in your family, or in your schooling. You will probably be active and working right up to the end of your days. You will have either exceptionally good or exceptionally bad relationships with your brothers and sisters. Your own adult home will be full of books, music and people, and you may run some kind of business from it. You need freedom to come and go, but the home you return to will be spacious and full of expensive furniture and equipment.

Cancer
Your early experiences will have a strong impact on your future development. You should remain close to your parents throughout their lives. Your adult home will be very important to you and, even though you frequently travel away from it, you see it as a safe haven. You may work partially or wholly from your home. You may enjoy cooking, and your kitchen should be very well equipped. You could collect odds and ends, antiques or even junk.

Leo
Your early days could have been very difficult, either because you were over-disciplined or because your parents lived a nomadic existence. Later on, you try to make a traditional and comfortable home, but even this may become disrupted in some way. You may want a nice home but somehow find that you are prevented from spending a lot of money on it. If you entertain you will do so in style and if you work from home you will make sure that you have all the latest equipment to hand.

Virgo
Your early life could have been difficult, either in the home or at school. However, your home environment was full of books and music. Your parents would have placed a bit too much importance on good behaviour, a 'proper' diet and cleanliness, and too little on how you felt. Your adult home is spacious and comfortable, with a well-stocked kitchen. If you work from home, you will have all the latest communications equipment.

Libra
Your early life would have been calm, pleasant and loving, with nice surroundings and respectable parents. Your adult home should be large and very comfortable, full of artistic objects and music. You probably like cooking, so your kitchen will be well-equipped, but any entertaining which you do will be on a small scale.

Scorpio
The circumstances of your birth may have been strange, and there could have been some kind of conflict raging in the family at the time you were born. The atmosphere in your childhood home may have been tense and uncomfortable. Your adult home would be far more pleasant, with an emphasis on good food and a comfortable lifestyle, but you must guard against tension creeping in even there. You may find that you spend a good deal of time alone in your home, either by choice or by circumstances.

Sagittarius
Your early life may have been peculiar, either because your parents were heavily involved in religious activities or because they were immigrants from another culture. You may have lived in two worlds at the same time. Your adult home will be pleasant and open, not over-tidy, but full of interesting knick-knacks. You may work from home or use it as a base to travel away from.

Capricorn
Your childhood home may have been happy although lacking in material comforts or it may have been a source of tension and stress. You would have been encouraged to work hard for material success. Your latter days will be very comfortable and you could well end up being very rich. Your adult home will be well-organized and filled with valuable goods, but you may decide to keep animals in preference to having children.

Aquarius
During childhood, your life at home or school may have been very unsettled or even eccentric. Your adult home could also be rather strange, either being very sumptuous and filled with

expensive goods and gadgets, or filled with an odd assortment of junk. Alternatively, your furniture and equipment could be ultra modern. You may work from your home part of the time, but whether this is so or not, your home is often filled with friends and neighbours.

Pisces

There may have been some mystery surrounding the circumstances of your birth or alternatively, you might have been brought up in a nomadic sort of family. Both your childhood home and your later adult one will reflect the many interests of the people who live in it. These may include books and equipment associated with the occult, magic, religion or travel. Your surroundings may be deliberately 'different', perhaps arty, musical, or earth-motherish. Your children will have a good deal of freedom, but they may not actually communicate much with you.

CHAPTER 17

Cusps

A cusp is the point where one sign ends and the next begins. We know that to be 'born on a cusp' means that the Sun is located at the very beginning or end of a sign and this can lead to a blending of both signs in the personality. For example, someone who was born with the Sun at 29° of Pisces would have a certain amount of Aries energy and enterprise added to their withdrawn and reflective Pisces nature. When the ascendant is 'cuspy', the situation is different. If the ascendant is close to the beginning of a sign, most of the first house will be the same sign; this makes the effect of the ascendant very strong. Figure 5 shows how this looks on a chart.

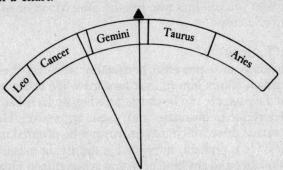

Figure 5: A strong ascendant sign.

If the ascendant is close to the end of a sign the situation becomes cloudy, because the ascendant will be in one sign while the first house straddles the cusp and then spreads itself out over a large area of the next sign. Figure 6 shows how this situation looks on a chart.

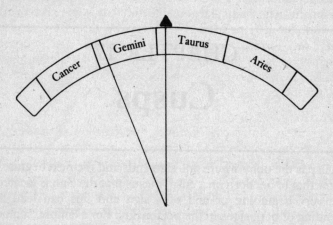

Figure 6: A weak ascendant sign

To add to this confusion, I have an entirely personal theory which deviates from normal astrological thinking. I believe that cusps have a life of their own which goes beyond the simple blending of the two signs which are involved. To test this theory, take a look at the list of cusps below and apply my ideas to anyone who you can find who has the Sun, Moon or Ascendant on or over a cusp.

Aries/Taurus
This belongs to a powerful personality who has the kind of vision which allows him to look forward while retaining strong links to the past. He can be charming when he feels like it, but is also determined, obstinate and even aggressive. He has a strong sexual drive which may or may not be diverted into other activities. He is probably interested in the arts or music and also in architecture and any kind of lasting achievement. He could be a powerful, visionary leader, or a complete mess. Two examples

which are different in nature although similar in the kind of arena in which their lives have been lived out are Adolf Hitler and Queen Elizabeth the Second.

Taurus/Gemini

This person can be a creative dreamer, a self-indulgent type of personality who wants the good life and may even make an effort to work for it if pressed. He should be dexterous especially where any form of engineering is concerned. Travel interests him but so does his work, his home and the support of his family. He may move and talk slowly but his mind is quick and shrewd.

Gemini/Cancer

This person is moody, difficult to understand and probably too idealistic for his own good. He is a good listener and also a good talker but his idealism doesn't extend to leaving himself short of money; indeed he has the mind of a creative accountant. Complex; honest but devious, kind but mercenary, independent but desperate for a good relationship; both a mixer and a loner. He may always be on the move, looking for the most advantageous mixture of circumstances. He may carry a chip on his shoulder about past hurts or suffer from a low level of self-esteem.

Cancer/Leo

This subject wants to make a splash; he wants to be noticed and respected but he may be too lazy to achieve this ambition. If he really can't face too much work, he will try to marry someone who has a good income instead. He is probably quite artistic and certainly creative. He has a talent for working in the financial field and may be an excellent accountant or insurance salesman. He may be an excellent sales person as he genuinely likes people, especially young people.

Leo/Virgo

This subject is nervy, a high achiever who never thinks he has done enough. He can become ill when things go wrong or he can punish himself unnecessarily. Emotionally vulnerable, slow to grow up or accept change, he needs to gain confidence. He also needs a stable family life. He is kind hearted and good to others, especially his own family and friends.

Virgo/Libra
This subject is highly sexed and highly charged with many other kinds of energy as well. He enjoys work, especially if it gives him a chance to manage others, and he may travel extensively in connection with his work. He is clever, dexterous and a high achiever, a clever negotiator and a fascinating person, but is not easy to live with. He may dabble at things rather than work properly.

Libra/Scorpio
There may be something physically wrong with this subject, his spine and legs could be affected in some way, even to the point of semi-paralysis. Despite any disability, he overcomes everything and goes on to have an interesting career, often in some form of teaching or media work. This subject is a fighter who goes after what he wants. His marriage and other family or close relationships are likely to be excellent but he may choose not to have children. His outer manner is quite unpleasant on first acquaintance and he needs to work on this if he wishes to increase his popularity out in the world.

Scorpio/Sagittarius
This subject can be very mystical or spiritual in outlook, with a strong desire to help others. He seems to suffer more than most and puts up with it for longer than he really should. He is a reliable and hard worker who will stick to a job until the finish but he likes variety in his work and doesn't mind travelling in order to earn his money. This subject can suffer from accidents to the legs but he seems to overcome everything and keep going. He may be drawn to work in the fields of medicine or religion.

Sagittarius/Capricorn
This subject is fascinated by the occult and may be very psychic; he puts this fascination to use for the benefit of others. He can be very businesslike one minute but quite scatty and unrealistic the next. He needs to relax and have fun as he can find himself

on a treadmill of work. He draws the kind of family and friends to him who depend upon him to keep them happy and give them a good life, but he may get little back in return. He is suspicious of others which makes him prefer the company of his family to that of friends.

Capricorn/Aquarius

A strange mixture; outwardly competent and often sarcastic to the point of being offensive, but at the same time idealistic and kind hearted. He is very good to his family and close friends but is often too involved with work to spend much time with them. This subject either identifies himself with his work or he may be heavily involved with committee work. Muddle-headed and somewhat messy administratively, he is at his best when teaching or helping others. His ideas are often wonderful, very clever and truly workable.

Aquarius/Pisces

This subject is a mystic with strong leanings towards religion and/or the occult. He is a terrific teacher with the ability to inspire others. His vision is tremendous, but his ability to cope with day-to-day life may be completely lacking. He is impractical and may get himself into financial muddles. He may be very eccentric and faddy about everything from food, to clothing and the way he lives. To quote a remark made by my friend, Denise, 'such people are fascinating, but out-with-the-fairies!'

Pisces/Aries

Quite a number of people who have this cusp strongly marked on their charts choose to work in the professional astrological or psychic world. Their mixture of superb intuition coupled with their commercial instincts can make them very successful in almost any field of endeavour. However, their high ideals can make them hard to live with.

CHAPTER 18
Decanates

Each sign of the zodiac is divided into 30° which can be broken down into three groups of 10°. These sub-sections are called decans or decanates. The first decanate of any sign is ruled by its own sign, the second one is sub-ruled by the next sign along in the same triplicity and the third decanate is sub-ruled by the last sign in the same triplicity. For example, the sign of Aquarius is an air sign. The first decanate is sub-ruled by Aquarius itself, the second by Gemini also an air sign and the third by Libra the other air sign.

Figure 7: The Aquarius decanates

The influence of the decanates
I'm not sure that decanates are terribly important in themselves but they can have a subtle subsidiary influence on a birthchart. An interesting side issue is to look at your own family's charts

and see how the decanates fit together. For instance, I have the Sun in Leo in the third decanate which is sub-ruled by Aries while my father was born with the Sun in Aries in the second decanate which is sub-ruled by Leo.

I have suggested a few key ideas here but you can make up your own list if you prefer.

Aries/Aries	Pure Aries.
Aries/Leo	Leo adds dignity, stability and creativity.
Aries/Sagittarius	Sagittarius adds high-minded idealism, optimism, popularity and political aspirations.
Taurus/Taurus	Pure Taurus.
Taurus/Virgo	Virgo adds an aptitude for hard work and service to others but diminishes the Taurean confidence.
Taurus/Capricorn	Capricorn adds patience, acumen and ambition but also some pessimism and sadness.
Gemini/Gemini	Pure Gemini.
Gemini/Libra	Libra adds charm, calmness, a love of beauty and sex appeal.
Gemini/Aquarius	Aquarius adds academic ability, high-mindedness and eccentricity.
Cancer/Cancer	Pure Cancer.
Cancer/Scorpio	Scorpio adds determination, ambition, depth of feelings and an interest in health or healing.
Cancer/Pisces	Pisces adds vulnerability, mys-

	ticism, self-sacrifice and emotionalism.
Leo/Leo	Pure Leo.
Leo/Sagittarius	Sagittarius adds high-mindedness, the need to explore and sporting ability.
Leo/Aries	Aries adds impulsiveness, bossiness and independence.
Virgo/Virgo	Pure Virgo.
Virgo/Capricorn	Capricorn adds ambition, executive ability, practicality and patience.
Virgo/Taurus	Taurus adds calmness, practicality and an artistic eye.
Libra/Libra	Pure Libra.
Libra/Aquarius	Aquarius adds intellect, independence and political ability.
Libra/Gemini	Gemini adds speed of thought and action, wit, dexterity and intellect. ·
Scorpio/Scorpio	Pure Scorpio.
Scorpio/Pisces	Pisces adds vulnerability, self-sacrifice and an interest in health or healing.
Scorpio/Cancer	Cancer adds shrewdness, a need to care for others and a desire for stable family life.
Sagittarius/Sagittarius	Pure Sagittarius.
Sagittarius/Aries	Aries adds impulsiveness, courage, enterprise and sporting ability.

Sagittarius/Leo	Leo adds stability, love of children and animals, also arrogance.
Capricorn/Capricorn	Pure Capricorn.
Capricorn/Taurus	Taurus adds a love of beauty, music and the countryside together with a need for personal comfort.
Capricorn/Virgo	Virgo adds acumen, analytical or accounting ability, speed of movement and dexterity.
Aquarius/Aquarius	Pure Aquarius.
Aquarius/Gemini	Gemini adds speed of thought and action, mental agility and communication ability.
Aquarius/Libra	Libra adds calmness, sociability and a love of beauty.
Pisces/Pisces	Pure Pisces.
Pisces/Cancer	Cancer adds a need to care for others and a love of family life, but also shrewdness and determination.
Pisces/Scorpio	Scorpio adds stability and determination, plus an interest in psychology, medicine, and mysticism.

CHAPTER 19

Planets in Conjunction with the Ascendant

―――**Planets On or Near the Ascendant**―――

Here are some points which the more technically-minded readers might like to consider:

1. Planets which are in the first house have a strong influence on the subject's life and personality. If there is only one planet in this house or close to the ascendant, it will be strongly emphasized. If there is a group of planets, then the first house, and the sign which it occupies, will be stressed. The same could be said for planets in the twelfth house if they are close to the ascendant, except for the Sun which is a little dim in this house.

2. The planet nearest to the ascendant is called the *rising planet*. If there is nothing in the first house, but a planet is situated in the twelfth house very close to the ascendant, then that planet could be termed a rising planet. Please note that in this case the planet would have to be very close to the ascendant; for instance, no more than a degree or two away from it.

3. A planet which is in conjunction with the ascendant is vitally important, both in its effect on the personality, and in its effects on the subject's life. In some cases, a rising planet can be almost as important as the Sun in a birthchart.

If you know that you have a planet close to the ascendant, read the following information and see whether you agree that it influences your life strongly or not.

Sun conjunct ascendant

Assuming that the Sun and the ascendant are in the same sign, (e.g. Sun in Libra, Libra rising), that sign would become an ultra important factor on the chart. If the Sun and ascendant were in adjoining signs (e.g. Sun in Libra, Virgo rising), both signs would be emphasized, but not as much as if only one sign was involved. Transits and progressions over that part of the chart would be exceptionally noticeable. Assuming that the two factors were in the same sign, there would be no need for the ascendant to act as a shield to the personality. This pre-supposes a confident, outgoing, well-integrated person whose childhood experiences were encouraging. If the sign involved were a difficult one (Virgo, Capricorn or Gemini for instance), the childhood might have been hard, but the subject would have the inner strength to rise above the problems and could achieve a good deal of success in spite of them – or maybe because of them.

The subject who has the Sun and ascendant in conjunction has a powerful personality and a strong need to express himself in day-to-day life. He puts his own personal stamp on everything he does and he cannot live or work in a subservient position. He (or she) is strong and healthy, with good powers of recovery from illness. There may be problems in connection with his back or heart, but he would be able to overcome them more successfully than many others. His ego is involved in all that he does and any new beginnings will be initiated by himself, rather than by others. If he finds himself in the hands of fate (or in the hands of other people), he turns the situation to his own advantage as quickly as possible. This subject will have a sunny personality. He will be arrogant and difficult to deal with until he learns to restrain himself and re-channel his powerful energies. In an otherwise introverted or other-worldly chart this Sun placement injects energy, dynamism, cheerful optimism and self-centredness.

Moon conjunct ascendant

The Moon represents the emotions and reactions, therefore this placement denotes a sensitive and vulnerable nature. The feelings are close to the surface and are easily brought into play. The subject reacts in an intensely personal way to every stimulus and he links in easily to the feelings of others. The ideas, experiences and emotions of the mother will have a profound effect, and the subject will remain close to her, perhaps remaining involved in her life and her work for many years. It is even possible that the subject can remember the things which happened to his mother (and to him), before he was born. Childhood experiences and early training remain in the subject's unconscious mind throughout his life.

There is a strong need to create a home and family as well as to look after others by working in one of the caring professions. The subject may wish to protect the environment, preserve places, buildings and objects from the past, and also to create a better, kinder and safer future for mankind. Psychic ability is almost always present with this placement; there may even be vestigial memories of previous lives. All forms of intuition will be well developed.

The subject may be drawn to a career in travel, especially sea travel. Alternatively, he may wish to run a small business for himself. He is interested in history and tradition, and may try to revive traditional crafts or to collect fine things from the past. He will be able to retreat from the rat race from time to time, in order to calm himself and recharge his emotional batteries. Oddly enough, the Moon is associated with work in the public eye, or for the public good, so he may become a well-known 'personality'.

Being sensitive, he can become depressed or downhearted and may absorb the unhappiness of others. He must take care because this kind of 'psychic absorption' can make him ill. In a notably macho or materialistic chart, this Moon placement lends introspection and sensitivity to the needs and feelings of others.

Mercury conjunct ascendant

Mercury is concerned with communications and the mentality,

therefore these subjects are fluent talkers and good communicators. The subject may be highly intelligent or merely bright; active and street-wise. He will choose to work in a job which is directly involved with communications. My cousin, Brian, for example, has Virgo rising with Mercury close to the ascendant in the first house; he has worked as a salesman, tour guide and taxi driver, and is now in the business of selling advertising space. He is communicating with those who wish to communicate!

This subject is a logical thinker and an active worker. He may switch off from time to time, to allow his mind to relax. He is dutiful towards his parents and his family. He feels happy if his work is appreciated and miserable if it is not. This type of subject is restless, easily bored, interesting to listen to, humorous and sometimes very sarcastic. He suffers from nervous ailments when placed under pressure. In a stodgy or over-practical chart, this Mercury placement would add quickness of mind, curiosity and restlessness.

Venus conjunct ascendant

This confers good looks and a pleasant social manner. The subject may have a good singing voice, but even if this is not the case, he will at least have a very pleasant speaking voice. This placement of Venus adds refinement and a dislike of anything which is ugly, dirty or vulgar. This person may take a job in a field where he can create beauty in some way, for example as a gardener, furniture designer, hairdresser or dancer. If he doesn't get the opportunity to express his delight in creating beauty through work, he will take up an artistic or attractive hobby. The subject may be a good arbitrator, with a natural desire to create harmony and understanding all around him. He uses his attractive personality to help him in his day-to-day work.

This subject is materialistic. He enjoys making money and spending it on attractive and valuable goods. He is also concerned about values, both in terms of getting value for money and also in terms of personal values and priorities. He is unwilling to sacrifice anything which he values for the sake of others. Venus on the ascendant can add placidity and pleasantness to an otherwise forceful, dynamic or neurotic chart.

Mars conjunct ascendant

This adds impulsiveness, enterprise and courage to the character. The subject has a strong will and a fierce temper. This 'tough-guy' type can make things happen where other less courageous souls would prefer to run away and hide. This aggressive person stands out in a crowd, dominating and possibly bullying those around him. His influence extends to any sphere in which he becomes involved, and he can become a highly successful, fast-moving achiever. He is best suited for a position of leadership or, if he is too difficult for others to work under, as a self-employed entrepreneur. If the rest of the chart endows sympathy, co-operation and diplomacy, he can really reach the top. To my mind, this typifies the red-haired, red-faced, rugged 'where there's muck there's money' type of businessman. In an otherwise timid, stodgy or lazy chart, this can add enterprise, enthusiasm, energy and will-power.

Jupiter conjunct the ascendant

This adds joviality to the personality because the influence of this planet is cheerful, broadminded and outward looking. The subject is attractive to look at, with a sunny smile and good teeth. This placement adds the kind of broad frame and comfortable shape which looks great on a man, but is unfashionable nowadays for a woman. The subject's outer manner is cheerful, optimistic and confident, he carries authority well and he can be an inspirational leader without throwing his weight about. This subject is not likely to be biased against any class or colour of person and he is not the slightest bit snobbish, but he is highly intolerant of phonies and posers.

Traditionally, this placement gives a love of travel and exploration, plus a touch of studiousness. This person may be particularly interested in philosophy and metaphysical subjects. The subject should also be a lucky gambler, in business perhaps, rather than on the horses. His mind is good, and he can usually see both sides of any argument, but when he chooses to argue a point he becomes very attached to his own opinions. The chances are that the subject will become well-known in his particular field because he enjoys being in the public eye. He is likely to be in contact with many people as a result of working in a personnel, sales or marketing capacity. He could take up a career as a politican, church minister or lawyer if the rest of the chart leans that way. Education is another career possibility because there is a desire to influence others in a beneficial manner.

I have noticed that people who have this planet rising experience quite drastic ups and downs where money is concerned. They are invariably attractive, but the optimism which the old time astrologers associate with this planet can be dampened if there is a good deal of water on the chart. Nevertheless, this placement adds a touch of enterprise, luck and vision to an otherwise stodgy or earthbound chart. Jupiter rising subjects do seem to travel widely, often in connection with their work, and some eventually leave their country of origin altogether.

Saturn conjunct the ascendant
This placement is a real stinker! To be honest, I don't entirely share most astrologers' pessimistic attitudes towards Saturn. On the contrary, I see it as a stabilizing factor on many charts but, when it is on the ascendant or any of the angles for that matter, it takes a lot of living with. This planet brings insecurity, even fear; particularly during childhood. For some reason, the subject's sense of self-worth is crushed by circumstances during his childhood and he has to work long and hard to rebuild it. He may have been rejected by either (or both) of his parents, or deprived of their love and attention due to tragic events. If he was cared for by other people during his childhood he would have been aware that this was done on sufferance. He hides his real needs and feelings and may even deny himself the right to have any needs other than those which other people consider suitable. His natural creativity may be squashed because it doesn't fit in with the requirements of those around him. Depending upon the rest of the chart, this childhood can cause the subject to develop a hard and aggressive attitude to others later in life or on the other hand, he may allow himself (or herself) to become, and to remain a doormat, never making even the most reasonable kind of demands upon others. Another

possibility is that he rises above this unpromising start and becomes an outstanding success.

This person is reliable and responsible; he takes all commitments very seriously, he finishes all that he starts and his self-discipline is incredible. He may project an austere image, but underneath will be surprisingly idealistic and, in personal and family life, he is kindly, sensitive and thoughtful, while being tolerant of the foibles of others. His reserve may be hard to penetrate, although this would be mitigated by an otherwise outgoing type of chart. Any appearance of hardness or unfriendliness is caused by shyness and a fear of being hurt. This individual is uncomfortable in social situations, although relaxed with his family and close friends. However, he is frequently most comfortable at work. I guess that it's not surprising that many Saturn influenced people are workaholics.

Traditionally, Saturn on the ascendant or in hard aspect to it (e.g. in opposition or square) at the time of birth indicates a difficult birth. My own theory is that this planet, which is so associated with old age, denotes at least one important previous incarnation and it may be the memory of this which holds the subject back when it is time for him to be re-born. He just may not want to face the whole business again. Another interesting theory is that the mother had to work very hard while the child was young, which gave him an especially diligent parental role model.

As it happens, I was born with Saturn about one degree behind the ascendant and, although my childhood and early life were hard, things are much better now. Saturn is often close to the ascendant in writer's charts, I guess it gives us the necessary self-discipline to get the job done. This placement adds stability, thoroughness, patience and modesty to an otherwise neurotic, unpredictable, lazy or self-indulgent chart.

Uranus conjunct the ascendant

This adds a touch of eccentricity. The subject may be idealistic, unpredictable and quite fascinating. His interests will be unusual; he may be drawn to the world of astrology and the occult, if the rest of the chart has similar leanings. Humanitarian and broad-minded, he tends to opt for an unusual way of life, either following unusual beliefs or making his own up as he goes along. His life takes peculiar twists and turns, partly because he is prey to unusual circumstances and partly because he cannot stand too much normality. He has a good mind which is directed towards the unusual. He may be cranky, strange or visionary in his thinking whilst at the same time being stubborn and determined. The amount of individuality and unusualness will depend on the structure of the rest of the chart. Even an extremely mundane chart will be enlivened by this placement.

Neptune conjunct the ascendant
This fascinating planet can make the subject into an inspired artist, glamorous film star or a complete nut-case. The subject's childhood may have been strange and there could have been some kind of mystery surrounding his birth and parentage. It is possible that one of his parents was very peculiar, even to the extent of being mentally ill. The subject is sensitive, vulnerable, easily hurt and 'destroyed', and he may never have a clear idea of his own needs and feelings. He may try to run his life to someone else's rules, discovering later perhaps, that the rules he tried to follow were abnormal or twisted in some way.

This placement can make the subject psychic, mediumistic, and/or prone to fantasies. In extreme cases, he may lose track of reality altogether. Bear in mind the rest of the chart when Neptune is rising because if it is practical and sensible this will simply add artistry and sensitivity rather than genuine lunacy. The subject may be drawn to a career in the arts, photography, music or the mediumistic side of the occult. He will have a soft spot for anyone or anything which he sees suffering and could either work hard for some kind or charity organization or just be a collector of lame ducks.

Pluto conjunct the ascendant
This subject has great self-control and may seek to control, direct and guide the lives of others. This directing instinct could take him into the world of medicine, the media or teaching, depending upon the shape of the rest of the chart. In personal relationships he could be coercive or domineering and will try to

control his partner, either financially or sexually. His own personality is so controlled that it is hard to work out just what he is thinking or what really motivates him. Although very pleasant to the people he works with, he may be very difficult to live with and also something of a loner with no real friends. He is slow to grow up, but when he does he becomes a reliable adult who will never renege on any of his commitments. He is happiest in a career where he is in charge of others, and even happier if he can improve the lives of large numbers of people. He has an exceptionally sharp mind and the kind of insight which may make him uncomfortable to be near. He can pick up even the mildest of undercurrents and 'vibes', and always knows when someone doesn't really like him. He may well appear mild, gentle and amenable but when challenged or hurt, the 'Clark Kent' image vanishes and Superman appears in its place.

His virtues are tenacity and obstinacy, which have the effect of making him extremely reliable and dependable. He finishes all that he starts and does it properly. He arrives in good time for appointments, alert and properly equipped to do what is required of him. He hates to let go of anyone or anything but he will not allow anyone to shackle him or dictate to him. He must be able to come and go as he pleases.

This subject can be idealistic, paternalistic and very sensitive to the needs of others. He tries to improve the world he lives in wherever he can but, altruistic as he is, he cannot explain his motives to others and therefore may sometimes be misunderstood. He has an urge to heal those who are sick at heart or ailing physically, therefore he may choose to work in the medical field. Alternatively, he may help out on a part-time basis as a para-medic. Hypnotherapy might appeal to him, or he may use some of his spare time to work as a spiritual healer.

This planet adds sexuality. Depending upon circumstances and the rest of his chart, he may accept this side of his personality, use it and enjoy it, or he may block it out and try to drive his sexual needs and desires from his mind. If he denies his high-octane sexual needs he may become embittered or depressed. If he can explore this side of his nature he will relax, become comfortable with his strange, obsessive personality, and go on to lead a full and happy life. This placement will add depth and intensity on all levels to an otherwise superficial chart.

CHAPTER 20

Rectification

The term rectification refers to the hunt for an ascendant when the subject doesn't know his time of birth. Every astrology book which I have seen says that this is a job for a skilled astrologer, but even the most skilled astrologer has to start somewhere so why shouldn't you have a go too? There are various ways in which a chart can be rectified. The Aquarian Press publishes a whole book on this subject but, in the meantime, here are a few tips which may prove helpful to the novice.

When the birthtime is given approximately
If your subject gives you an approximate birthtime, for example, between about two and three o'clock in the afternoon, your best bet is to make up a chart for 2.30 p.m. and then try 'fine-tuning' the chart as described a little further along in this chapter.

Dowsing
If a birthtime is completely unknown you could try dowsing, but if you are not into psychic and mystical ideas you will need to find somebody who is. (Rectification dowsers advertise their services occasionally in national astrological magazines). The dowser holds a divining pendulum over each sign while tuning in psychically to his spiritual guides and also to his inner self. Eventually he will come up with a 'yes' movement on his pendulum. This may categorically point to one particular sign,

or it might point to two opposing signs, thereby showing the ascendant/descendant axis.

If you feel happier with science, technology, and psychology, then dowsing will not appeal much to you. However, if you already read Tarot, or have mediumistic abilities, you could well become skilled at this line of work.

When the subject has no idea when he was born

It is possible to work out a rising sign by a process of elimination. This is not easy and it requires a thorough knowledge of the energies and characteristics of each rising sign. Firstly, put the chart together or at least list the planets in their signs so that you can see which influences are already in existence on the chart before you begin to hunt for the rising sign. If this points to an obvious type of personality and a specific kind of childhood, then even at this stage some rising signs will begin to fit better than others. If the subject does not resemble his Sun sign, then try to work out what sign he does resemble – the chances are that he will be projecting his rising sign. The second step is to ask a few questions about the childhood and background. The following suggestions may prove helpful.

If the subject was the eldest child or the most responsible one in the family, he may have been Cancer, Leo, Capricorn, Scorpio or even Aquarius on the Ascendant. If he was the youngest or the least likely to take the lead, this would point towards Gemini, Virgo, Sagittarius or Pisces.

If he was loved just because he existed, without having to prove himself to his parents, then his rising sign could be Cancer, Leo, Libra, Sagittarius, Capricorn or Aquarius. If he was only approved of, or even loved, because he behaved in an acceptable manner, or passed exams to order, then he could have Virgo, or Pisces rising.

If he really didn't fit in anywhere as a child he may have had Aries, Gemini or Scorpio rising.

Closeness to the mother (or other nurturing figures), would be shown by Taurus, Cancer, Libra and Capricorn; while closeness to the father would indicate Taurus, Leo, Capricorn and Aquarius. A love/hate relationship with one (or both) of the

parents might point to Scorpio or Pisces. Parents who were not
interested in the child and fobbed him off with things rather
than love suggest Taurus, Leo, Libra, possibly Scorpio or
Sagittarius.

A cautious, shy approach during childhood would be shown
by a feminine/negative sign on the ascendant, while an
extroverted child or one who was expected to act in an extrovert
or even rather macho manner, would be Aries, Gemini, Leo or
Sagittarius.

If by this process of elimination, you come up with two
possible signs, make up two charts with the ascendant placed in
the middle section of each of the two signs and then have a go at
some fine tuning.

Pre-natal epoch birthcharts

This method was demonstrated to me by Douglas Ashby who
had, in turn, been shown how it works by Chryss Craswell.

This idea appears at first glance to be even crazier than
dowsing, but it works! In fact, it was by a process of pre-natal
epoch work, elimination and finally, fine tuning, that my own
ascendant was found. The method is based on the premise that
a normal pregnancy takes 280 days or 40 weeks, so it will only
work if the subject was born fairly naturally, after a normal
length of pregnancy. To find the pre-natal chart, count back 40
weeks (or 280 days) from the date of birth. This will take you
back, more or less, to the date of conception. Look at the
position of the Moon on the conception date because this will be
located on, or around, either the potential ascendant or
descendant.

Fine tuning

This can be done in two ways. The first is by moving the
mid-heaven backwards and forwards. The MC moves at
roughly a degree for a year, therefore events can be pin-pointed
by the aspects it makes to other planets on the natal chart as it
progresses. The subject can be asked to mention any
particularly memorable events in his childhood and the rectified
mid-heaven can be swung backwards and forwards until it
connects with one of the planets or some other feature on the

chart at the relevant age. For example, a change in one's direction in life would connect with a progression of the mid-heaven from one sign to another. An accident might be set off by a mid-heaven square to Mars or Uranus. Good exam results might be mid-heaven conjunct, sextile or trine Mercury, while a move of house would connect with the Moon, with a square or opposition, if the subject felt it to be an unhappy event or with a trine or sextile if it was a happy one. A conjunction could go either way. Obviously, this takes a good deal of astrological knowledge, but there are plenty of books on the market which show the effect of planets natally, by progression or when transitting.

Even more fine tuning

The final step is to look back in time at the movement of planets as shown in the ephemeris (or on the computer). Ask the subject what was happening at the times when planets crossed the angles (asc., dsc., MC and IC). A Jupiter transit across the mid-heaven can bring a terrific expansion in the area of one's work, public life and status. If the mid-heaven is in a creative sign, such as Pisces or Taurus, this can bring a surge of creativity and recognition for one's work. Saturn crossing the ascendant will cause a slowing down of one's life and a feeling of being restricted and over-burdened with responsibilities. This will last for a couple of years as it transits through the first house, possibly bringing a period of depression and also hard work, resulting in worthwhile long term gains and a definite re-structuring of one's life. If a subject marries under this kind of transit the marriage would be to an older person and/or be based on a need for material security. Venus transits might cause the subject to fall in love, or to become more aware of beauty and harmony. It would also cause the subject to re-evaluate his priorities in life. Marriage resulting from sexual attraction could be due to Mars, Pluto or even Uranus.

I know that rectification is difficult. It really does help if you use a computer because a dozen or more charts might need to be made up in the hunt for the ascendant. It is even necessary to make up separate charts for various times in the subject's past,

as they will show by both progression and transit what was going
on at that time of his life. If you set these up for those times
which were the turning points in the subject's life and also for
times of exceptional joy or sadness, this will help in the
rectification procedure.

Now you know why the books recommend that you take this
problem to a skilled astrologer. I suggest that you take a pocket
full of money with you at the same time, because this is hard and
time-consuming work and nobody who has spent years of
studying astrology should be expected to do it for a pittance.
Work out what a highly-trained and skilled accountant or
solicitor might want for a few hours' work and give the
astrologer the same – he may be an idealist, but he's got to eat
and pay his bills too.

Glossary

Ascendant:	The actual degree of the zodiac sign which is rising up over the ecliptic at the time of birth.
Cusp:	The point where one sign adjoins the next.
Decanate:	A ten-degree segment of a sign.
House cusp:	The point where one house adjoins the next.
Houses:	The division of the chart into 12 segments, each segment is called a house.
IC:	Immum Coeli, sometimes called the nadir. The bottom of the chart, also the darkest point of night.
MC:	Medium Coeli or Mid-heaven.
Mid-heaven:	Also called the zenith or the meridian. This is the highest point in the sky at the time of birth. Also the top of the chart in some house systems.

Bibliography

Poppe Folly, *The New Astrology*, Pan, 1985.

Betty Lundsted, *Astrological Insights into Personality*, Astro Computing Services, San Diego, 1980.

Derek and Julia Parker, *The Compleat Astrologer*, Mitchell Beazley, 1971.

Julia Parker, *The Astrologer's Handbook*, Mitchell Beazley, 1980.

Carl L. Sargent, *The Astrology of Rising Signs*, Rider, 1986.